"We need to talk"

Tough Conversations with Your Kids

From Sex to Family Values
Tackle Any Topic with Sensitivity and Smarts.

RICHARD HEYMAN, ED.D.

Avon, Massachusetts

Published by
Adams Media, an F+W Media Company
57 Littlefield Street, Avon, MA 02322. U.S.A.
www.adamsmedia.com

ISBN 10: 1-59869-878-8
ISBN 13: 978-1-59869-878-7

Printed in the United States of America.

J I H G F E D C B A

Library of Congress Cataloging-in-Publication Data
is available from the publisher.

This publication is designed to provide accurate and authoritative
information with regard to the subject matter covered. It is sold with
the understanding that the publisher is not engaged in rendering legal,
accounting, or other professional advice. If legal advice or other expert
assistance is required, the services of a competent professional person
should be sought.
—From a *Declaration of Principles* jointly adopted
by a Committee of the American Bar Association
and a Committee of Publishers and Associations

Many of the designations used by manufacturers and sellers to distin-
guish their product are claimed as trademarks. Where those designations appear in this book and Adams Media was aware of a trademark
claim, the designations have been printed with initial capital letters.

This book is available at quantity discounts for bulk purchases.
For information, please call 1-800-289-0963.

Contents

Preface

"Where do babies come from?" your five-year-old son asks during his afternoon snack.

"Why do you want to know?" you reply, ducking a really tough question with another question.

"I just want to know."

"I thought I told you when your sister was born."

"I don't remember."

"I don't want to talk about it just now."

"Why?"

"I just need some time to think about it."

What's wrong with this picture? Is it that a five-year-old is interested in something to do with sex? Or is it that you think you can't answer his question without embarrassing yourself, so pass on it for the time being?

Of all the difficult topics of conversation that might come up for parents and children of any age, sexuality probably tops the list. That's why most parents try to avoid the topic completely and hope their kids will learn about it from someone else. But there is no shortage of other tough topics moms and dads, at sometime or other in their children's lives, will need to talk about: right and wrong, fighting, rules, drugs, death of a person or pet, children who are different, proper behavior toward the opposite sex, money, toys and clothes, schoolwork, choices and moral development, separation and divorce, money, alcohol, drugs, and cigarettes.

We Need to Talk: Tough Conversations with Your Kids is a clear and sympathetic guide through this mythical minefield of difficult conversations. I call it mythical because the truth is, any topic can be discussed with children of any age in an honest way, as long as parents carefully choose their words and examples and speak with the tone and tact befitting their child's age, gender, and ability to understand. Using vivid examples, expert commentary, and useful scripts, this book gives parents those words and examples and shows how to fit them to their own children, whether they are preschoolers, grade school children, or teens.

Introduction

Tone and Tact—Finding the Right Words for Your Child at Any Age

IF YOU THINK parents have trouble talking to their children about some topics more than others, you're right. But if you think that's because those topics are intrinsically too tough, you're wrong. Not only can every parent talk about any topic to any child, they can do it easily and truthfully. It doesn't matter if you're shy or bold, easily embarrassed or unshockable, Type A personality or Type B, woman or man, mother or father, extrovert or introvert. You just have to know what to say and how to say it.

Tough Talk with a Tough Teen—A True Story

My wife and I have three children, including a son who, when he was a child, wouldn't accept us as having any authority over him. Our other two children acknowledged us as their parents, listened to what we had to say, and did what we asked. We could talk to them about anything.

Our son argued with us over almost everything. He did poorly in school, but had lots of friends. As he grew up, he proved to be very inventive and very skilled with machines. However, by the time he reached eighteen he was neither in school nor working. We decided the best thing for him and for us was to ask him to leave home. Our problem was how to do it. What could we say to our child to get him to move out? More importantly, what could we do to get to him to understand our point of view and why we thought it would be better for him and for us if he made his own way? Since he had always rejected our authority and was of legal age, we felt he needed to be his own boss in his own apartment.

Our concern was that he understood we were doing this not because we wanted to but because we had to, for his sake; he needed to be responsible for his own life. We confronted him in his own room, my wife and I, and by the time we were finished we were both crying. This is roughly how the conversation went:

US: We're sorry, darling, but we think the time has come for you to move out. Right now you're using our house as a hotel. You're not working and you're not going to school. If you were, we'd be happy to have you live here as you always have and we'd support you. But you're not, so we think it would be best for you, and for us, if you moved out. We love you, but we need you to go.

We didn't want to sound unfeeling, but we needed to be firm. We both hated saying this, but we felt we had no choice. He was a seriously disruptive part of our family. We also wanted him to know he had options— school and or work.

HIM: So, what do you want from me?

He was never easy to have a conversation with and this, of course, was one he certainly didn't want to have—nor did we.

US: Just what we said: you have to leave.

We had both agreed beforehand that we wouldn't back down. If we did, things would never change for him, and would actually probably go from bad to worse. We were using what was called tough love, to be used only when all else fails.

HIM: Where can I go?

We knew he had some options, including a really close friend who had moved into his own apartment and whose father we knew very well.

US: You have lots of friends. What about moving in with Martin? We think you will be better off staying with him, if he'll let you.

HIM: What if he won't have me? Where do I go?

US: We'll help you look if you want.

And we would have, if it had been necessary. But we wanted this to be his first real taste of the freedom and responsibilities that come with being on your own.

HIM: How soon do you want me to leave?

This is where we started crying.

US: We'd like you to be out by the weekend if you can arrange it. We'll help you move if you need our help.

We didn't want to give him too much time or we were afraid we might back down, and that was something we didn't want to do.

HIM: Okay, I'll call Martin.

US: Okay, let's hope he'll have you. Please know that we love you very much; you're our son and we only want the best for you. But we can't go on this way and that's why you have to leave. If you ever decide you want to go back to school or if you get a job and need to live here, we'd welcome you back.

This was said through a veil of tears.

He did call Martin, who said yes. By Saturday, he was gone. For the next year, he shared his friend's apartment. We saw him occasionally, but kept in touch by phone as well.

In over forty years as a parent, and now grandparent, I've had thousands of conversations with children about every topic imaginable, from sex to drugs to school to work, from relationships to fighting. But none was ever as tough as that one. It was incredibly hard to do at the time, but my wife and I, and our son, think it turned out to be for the best.

Speaking with Tone and Tact

I once did some research on how teachers and children talked to and treated each other in school because I was interested in how good teaching and learning happen, even in difficult situations; how showing each other kindness and respect, two important parts of tone and tact, turns what could be a disruptive event into one creating solidarity. The class I observed and videotaped over the course of a year was in a hamlet in the Canadian Rockies. It was a grade-one class in a school not too distant from an Indian reservation.

This particular class turned out to be especially interesting because every child, except for one little girl, was from that reservation. They arrived each morning in buses and cars. School began promptly each morning at 8:30 A.M., and many of the children would be there by then. But the wonderful thing about this class and the teacher concerned the Native Canadian children who would continue to arrive throughout the morning. Each time a new child walked into the classroom, at 9:30 A.M. or 11:00 A.M., in the midst of lessons about reading, writing, or spelling, the teacher would stop what she was doing and welcome the child with a smile and a gracious "Thank you for coming." There were no recriminations, no hostility, no scolding this six- or seven-year-old for something far beyond her control. This brilliant young teacher showed only kindness and gratitude that the child had come at all.

I think of this example as illustrating perfect tone and tact because it shows great respect for the people involved, an understanding of the situation in all its complexity, and a talent for creating a positive, caring atmosphere, rather than a negative, hostile one.

What you say to your child is as important as how and when you say it. By conversational tone, I mean speaking in a voice that shows you love your child and value and understand your relationship with him. By conversational tact, I mean using words appropriate to your child's age and his understanding and range of knowledge and experience. It also means leaving some things unsaid, perhaps because your child is too young to understand, or too old to need those things made explicit.

Conversational tone and tact can't be faked; your child knows phony when she hears it. Even preschoolers know when mommy is pretending and show it in their inattention. Just as school children know when a teacher is really interested in them and when she is not, they know when a parent is just mouthing the words "I love you," "I understand," or "This is for your own good, not mine," and when a parent means it.

The following are some guidelines for talking with tone and tact to kids of any age. They embody some things I think of as eternal truths for talking to children—or anyone else—but I make them explicit here because they are truths we seem to easily forget when we have conversations with kids.

Tone—How to Say It

Speak from the heart as well as the head. Speaking to your ten-year-old son about divorcing his father can't be done without strong feeling. You know he will be confused and angry, just as you are. He may seem mature in so many ways, but this will not be one of them. No matter what the reason for separating and or divorcing, your son will only wish that you will work it out and stay together. Put yourself in your child's place. Imagine how your child hears what you're saying by trying to think and feel like someone his age. Whether he is four, ten, or fourteen, you need to offer messages of care, consolation, and understanding.

Make your tone suit your topic. The subject of sex, for example, should be approached in a number of different ways depending on your child's age. Your four-year-old needs a straightforward, factual explanation of sex, including the right words for body parts and sexual acts. An older child or teenager can understand more of the emotions, morality issues, societal constraints, and other more complicated aspects of sex.

Use your tone of voice to invite your child to talk. Your sensitive fifteen-year-old, whose closest friend just died in a car accident, needs to talk as well as listen. Your tone of speaking and listening needs to encourage her to talk about her feelings. One-way conversations about tough topics don't work. If you do all the talking and your child does all the listening, she may tune you out because you sound like a poor teacher whose tone of voice says only her words, ideas, opinions, and feelings are important.

Show that you are listening with respect and patience. Say your six-year-old tells you about his schoolmate's funny clothing and strange way of speaking. You want to encourage him to accept and enjoy differences among the children in his school and community.

You and he can't have a successful conversation about this without showing respect and patience as you listen to his story. You set this tone with the look on your face, your unswerving attention to his words, and the tone of your voice when you respond to his words. Show your child by word and deed that you value and need his input.

Be clear that this is an open-ended conversation. You talked to your daughter about the birds and the bees when she was three, then again when she was ten, and now you're doing it again as she reaches puberty. Tough conversations like these don't have clear beginnings, middles, and endings. You don't need to discuss everything in one conversation; your tone should imply this topic can and will be revisited. Then, you both have the option to probe the topic more deeply as new thoughts and feelings and needs arise.

Tone—How Not to Say It

Don't talk down to your child. Your son may be only five years old, but he has opinions on lots of matters that concern both of you directly, and he's not terribly happy when you talk to him like he is still a baby. You're better off assuming he knows more than you think he does. Your tone should show how much you value his understanding, at whatever level it might be. The key point is to know your child and talk appropriately. At any age, it's better to talk up than down. Judge what's appropriate by the way he responds.

Don't ignore your child's concerns. Throughout her young life, your daughter has come to you wanting to talk, to tell you stories from school or discuss concerns about sex, death, divorce, schoolwork, and now, drugs. Hopefully, you will always be happy to listen and talk about these things. Your child has legitimate concerns about these tough topics. Imagine what they may be and listen carefully as she expresses them, invited or uninvited. Then address them in a conversational way.

Don't yell at your child. Yelling solves no problems and sets the wrong tone for the talk. You may want to yell about your child's behavior in public or his poor work at school, but it won't help and will probably just hurt and make things worse.

Adults preach to children too often. "Do this," "Don't do that," and "Listen to me, I know best," are phrases children hear for much of their young lives. Preaching doesn't give your child a chance to join in the conversation; it implicitly devalues her input. Your daughter is a good girl and listens when you ask her to. Be careful not to take advantage of her good nature.

Your children have their own experiences that come from their everyday lives, just as you do—you don't have a monopoly on understanding life's highs and lows. Tough topics are successfully discussed when you and your child both contribute to the conversation. You take turns, you listen respectfully to each other, and you learn from each other. You decide what to say next by listening to what your child is saying now. You may find your answers in your child's words.

Tact—What to Say

Always ask yourself how your child will experience the conversation. You have just presented your three-year-old son with a baby sister. He wants to know if she will go back into your tummy. How do you tactfully tell him she's here to stay? Tact means being open to your child's experiences, which are both common and unique. You must accept both these aspects in order to be tactful in talking about tough topics, like sharing your love. You know you have more than enough for both children, but he doesn't. Constant physical love and reassuring actions need to reinforce anything you say about loving him as much as ever.

Your talk must show your child you see her as a subject, not an object. When your daughter asks why she has to do her homework when she desperately wants to watch a movie, you need to tie your answer to her as your daughter, not as just another teenager who wants to ignore her schoolwork. You need to talk to her knowing who she is, what her strengths and weaknesses are, and help her understand herself. Your talk needs to show a great sensitivity to your child's needs so you can talk about the importance of school in the context of her life, not just yours.

Sometimes you need to be subtle, no matter how tempted you are to bop your child on the head to make a point. Give him credit for understanding more than he can say. Don't belabor issues. Be playful, understated, subtle. Bop him on the head only as a last resort.

Show that you have confidence in your child. You have given your daughter some important jobs to do around the house; this shows you trust her and think she is mature enough to bear some of the responsibility for the smooth running of the household. Trust is an excellent teacher. Your confidence in your daughter will help build her self-confidence.

Go with the flow of the situation. You want to confront your son with the cigarettes you found in his jacket pocket when doing the laundry. How do you begin? There's no one way to do this. Your conversations about this tough topic can be scripted from your point of view, but your child won't have read your script. You have to be ready to improvise, go with the flow. If you listen carefully to what your son says, you will know what to say next. Above all, don't ignore his words and just follow your own agenda. Successful conversations must always be jointly created.

Tact—What Not to Say

Don't assume your child's personal space is always available to you. Your daughter has her own room, which may seem to you like a cesspit, littered with goodness knows what. Yet, it's her personal space and you, as her parent, need to respect it. Once children begin regular school, they need to be given more privacy and responsibility for their own space; beyond the age of six only matters of grave concern or harm should warrant you entering your child's space without her permission. Personal space can be mental as well as physical, so be tactful when probing for stories, answers to questions, and seeking information. You need to not only respect your child's space, but nurture and preserve it. She needs personal space every bit as much as you do.

Don't take advantage of your child's vulnerability. It is supremely tactless to criticize a child for not being as good at something as you are. Especially in areas like school or sports, children are especially vulnerable to comparisons with other children or their parents. Children are forming their own self and identity and need positive, not negative, reinforcement.

You may think something like separation anxiety is silly, but those fears feel very real to your child. All of us have fears—of heights, falling, dying, going broke, losing a loved one. Some are more reasonable than others, but all are real to the person who suffers from them. It would be extremely hurtful to deny these fears exist.

Don't use lots of negative words. Labels like "lazy" and "selfish" don't do anything to help the situation, however true they may be.

There are moments when every parent is fed up with their child's behavior and lets fly with some name calling. It might be satisfying for the moment, but in the long run it doesn't stop the behavior. Tact demands a positive approach in which words challenge rather than demean. Use expressions like "What if . . . ?" "How about . . . ?" "Why not . . . ?" and "Let's see . . ." to open the door for solutions.

Don't forget that the differences between boys and girls can make a difference. Christine, a fifteen-year-old, was incensed that her brother Mark, a fourteen-year-old, was allowed to walk home alone at night from a friend's house, while she was not. Christine was right to be angry. She wanted to know why girls have to be protected in ways that boys don't. What would your answer be? How can you tactfully explain something that Christine already knows but refuses to accept; that girls get attacked because they are so much more vulnerable and they are, to their attackers, objects of sexual fantasy, desire, and violence?

Any conversation about gender differences needs to honestly and tactfully take account of the fact that boys and girls develop physically and mentally at different rates, and their ways of understanding and acting upon the world differ. The principle of distributive justice tells us to treat equals equally and unequals unequally. You need to explain, tactfully, that for purposes of "treatment," boys and girls are often different, so treating them the same would be unjust, as well as unwise.

Parental Fears

In spite of all this talk about proper tone and tact in tough conversations with your child, you still have fears about having these talks.

What fears do many people have about such conversations? Here are twelve fears that top the list and how to overcome them:

- Fear of being embarrassed or embarrassing your child. In spite of what you think, children prize honesty from parents, and they can see right through dishonesty. You won't embarrass them or yourself if you're honest while at the same time trying to understand how they will experience your words.
- Fear of failing. Think of the price you and your child will pay if you don't have this conversation. If you do all this talking and nothing improves, nothing gets understood, the sharing doesn't happen, you have given it your best shot. Remember, you can't measure the effects of your talk right away; it takes time for things to be understood and to change.
- Fear of sounding too alarmist. If you don't want to blow things out of proportion, keep that fear in mind as you talk and use measured tone and tact. These are tough conversations, but remember that they don't mean the end of the world. Keep things in proportion.
- Fear of making matters worse. Talking about tough topics will only make matters worse if you forget why you're having the conversation. It's not for your sake; it's for your child's. Make it a two-way street—talk and listen carefully. Don't preach or think you have all the answers. Your child probably has most of them.
- Fear that you won't say the right things. We never know the right thing to say except in the actual situation. Let your child's talk tell you what the right thing to say is when it's your turn. The right thing is that which will make the most sense to your child.

- Fear of alienating your child even more. You can't control your child, but you can control yourself. Don't let this become a battle. You want a win-win situation and you can get that if you pay more attention to your child's needs than to your own. Take your cues from him or her. Don't push too hard and don't think you have to get everything accomplished in one try.
- Fear they will think you don't love them. Then don't criticize or pretend you have all the answers. Make this conversation a joint creation. It's talk about a tough topic, but your goal should be to create mutual understanding
- Fear they won't love you anymore. Speak from your heart as well as your head. If you have a good relationship with your child to begin with, then you won't risk losing her love simply because you're talking about a tough topic.
- Fear you might be too heavy handed. You might be. Many parents are when they start "talking about serious things" with their kids. Begin by smiling and keep that smile going. It's hard to be heavy-handed when you've got a nice smile on your face.
- Fear of hurting them. You won't hurt them if you keep them in mind all the time. Be positive in what you say, not negative. Start by talking about all the good things your child is just for being himself. Don't ever lose sight of the goodness of his essential being. This topic is just a ripple on the surface, not the whole stream or ocean.
- Fear of not being tough enough. Knowing your child intimately will help you decide how tough to be. Never lose sight of what you know about your child's age, gender, maturity, and level of understanding. These will guide you in choosing the right words and attitude.

- Fear of losing control. Don't make this a high-stakes game. Keep it light and friendly. If it's not a life or death issue, you must never use words that show anger or unnecessary alarm. Choose the right space for talking. Have your conversation outside in your garden or a park. Go for a walk. Do it in a public space where you must always consider those around you. And never forget that your child is the reason for this talk, not you.

Creating Great Relationships

This book is all about tough topics of conversation you will cover at some point or another in your relationships with your children. Most of these topics are serious in nature and should be approached in a serious way. However, you don't want to take this to the point of making these conversations feel like negative experiences. If you do this, your child will learn to shy away from any sort of conversation with you. Instead, you want to create a positive forum for discussion that might even include some laughter and silliness once in a while. The goal is to create a relationship of wonderful tone and tact between adult and child.

For most children, adults are always serious, all-knowing, and quite strict about not saying anything stupid. After all, parents want their children to know the right things to say and do and they want them to know the truth about the world. But being silly creates a world adults and children can share. By leveling the playing field, kids can compete for silliness equally with the grownups because kids wrote the book when it comes to being silly. At least that's what most adults and kids think: kids talk silliness and adults talk seriousness.

The truth is that tone and tact, properly understood and used, create great relationships and give you the ability to discuss any topic, tough or simple, with any children of any age in an honest way. Using tone and tact requires no special training or skill. Just remember that conversations on tough topics need to be done for your child's sake, not yours. You should leave your ego and self-importance behind. Simply work with your child on this one and smile. Nothing is ever a matter of life and death except matters of life and death. In this conversation, think of your child's age, gender, and ability to understand. Don't talk down, don't patronize, don't preach; just have a gentle conversation with your child as you would with a spouse or friend.

Chapter 1

Conversations about Reproduction and Sex

How do you talk about reproduction and sex with your kids? Just thinking about it probably makes you squirm. Your five-year-old daughter asks you where babies come from. Do you tell the truth? Your ten-year-old son tells you he has a crush on this girl and wants to know how to make her like him. Do you encourage him in his crush or advise him against it? Your fifteen-year-old daughter tells you she wants to start taking birth control pills. Your first thought is, "No way!" but then you start thinking about actions and consequences. What do you tell her?

With any luck, this chapter will help get rid of your sweaty palms, your fear of being honest, and your knee-jerk reactions, and will put you on the path to reasonable, honest talk with your kids about a difficult and critically important topic.

Conversations with Preschoolers

Your five year-old son is having his afternoon snack and suddenly asks where babies come from. Your immediate reaction is to avoid answering him because you don't know what to say or how to say it. Do you tell him the truth or do you stick to the old "stork" story? What words do you use? It's much too tough a subject, you think; better to let him learn it in sex education once he's in school.

But your better instincts kick in. You know your son; he's asking this question because he really wants to know. You've always made a point of answering your children's questions as honestly and truthfully as you could, using words and examples they could understand, and you've found from those experiences that your children know and understand much more than you think. So you decide to take on the challenge.

Talking to your preschoolers about reproduction needs this honesty. You're not looking to change their behavior, just to provide them with information they can store away for future use. Even at this young age, questions about where babies come from will make you think hard and reflect on how to best answer them so they go away with a full and healthy understanding appropriate to their age.

Your tact shows your special sensitivity to your child, the situation, and the topic of your talk. Be honest about reproduction, but don't say things preschoolers can't understand. You don't want to shock or confuse them, so some things are better left unsaid. Don't offend the innocence of your child, but don't belittle their intelligence and ability to understand, either.

Suit your words to your child's level of understanding and experience, neither talking down to her nor over her head. Your tone will show you are genuinely interested in talking about reproduction with her—she will sense if you are being less than that. Above all, honor and enjoy her curiosity and readiness to learn with a frank, open, and honest exchange of thoughts, feelings, and information.

Don't Miss this Opportunity

Your four- or five-year-old asks, "Where do babies come from?" Educators call this a "teachable moment," when children want to learn about something of their own volition. Your child wants to learn something about one of the most wonderful and miraculous events in life. Don't miss out on the chance to talk about it.

Preschoolers won't understand many of the emotional things associated with intercourse, pregnancy, and birth, but they can understand some of it. They can understand loving relationships that produced them. The rest will come when they're older and wiser, and when the hormones kick in.

If your child asks you to explain some aspect of human reproduction, do it right away, and do it using the right words, not slang. Put it in the context of love and relationships. You might think it's better to wait until your child is in school, where they will teach sex education, but it's even better if you start their education as soon as they start asking questions. Sex education in school is a good thing, but you can help make it certain that you child doesn't end up with a distorted, inaccurate understanding of sex from friends or popular culture.

How to Begin

Very young boys and girls notice that boys have penises and girls have vaginas, and you can teach them the proper names for these vital organs from the beginning. Talk about all the natural functions of our bodies while you're toilet training your children. Children in young families will very likely see their moms or their mom's friends pregnant. What an excellent opportunity to talk about the baby inside the mommy's tummy, how it's growing, and how it will be born, just as they grew inside their mommy and were born.

If your child asks how babies get into the mommy's tummy, tell him the truth. At this age, you can talk to children about reproduction without any embarrassment. For them it's just one more new thing to learn about life—it has no sexual or erotic baggage. Young children are sexual beings in a very different way from older children. It's more a matter of learning about personal identity: they rarely tire of pointing out that she's a girl and he's a boy, partly because young children don't have the concept of gender permanence. They don't know that she will always be a girl and he will always be a boy—that comes later.

Present sexual differences and reproduction in the context of love between moms and dads. Never criticize your child for the questions she asks. Answer honestly and openly using language appropriate for her age.

Accept your child's curiosity about genitalia and reproduction. Ask her if she knows the proper names for boys' genitalia and girls' genitalia. Ask her if she knows why boys and girls are different. Find books that show the differences and look at them together.

There are other sexuality issues you need to decide how to discuss. For example, you don't want your child to experience things impossible for him to understand at his age, like sexual adventures and exploration with young playmates or movies or shows or Internet sites that show sexuality far beyond their understanding. Use your child's comments and questions and other talks with him as your guide to what he should or should not see.

What to Say

Be honest. Tell your child that babies grow inside the mommy's tummy, in a special place called a womb where the baby feels warm and safe. Connect that to her own life inside mom's tummy.

Explain to her that boys and girls are different so that when they become men and women they can get married and have babies just like her. Don't shy away from the facts of reproduction. Preschoolers are quite ready to accept the fact that men and women need each other to have a baby, even if they don't really understand it. But always put it in the context of a mommy and daddy, because that they do understand.

Tell him that the daddy plants a little seed inside the mommy, where it grows until it's born. As long as you've already explained the anatomical differences between boys and girls, men and women, you can say that the daddy puts the seed into the mommy's tummy by putting his penis inside the mommy's vagina. The baby is born when it's fully grown and comes out of the mommy's tummy through the vagina. Recognize that this may sound very strange to your child. He may not believe it, but assure him that's the way babies are made and how they're born.

Be open with your child and assure her she can always ask you questions about this and that you'll always give her truthful answers. Explain that she'll understand this much better when she's ten or eleven.

This is not too much detail to tell a three-, four-, or five-year-old child. Your child may be amused, amazed, or unbelieving, but it's a really good way to teach him the truth about sexuality. The truth will serve him well as he grows up and hears all kinds of misinformation from other kids at school who haven't been told the truth. It will help him become a knowledgeable, respectful, and responsible adolescent and adult.

You needn't be afraid your child is going to run out and try to do this. It's not in her hormonal makeup at this age, and won't be for many years, by which time other factors, like social and religious mores, will help keep her natural urges in check insofar as that is possible or desirable.

The Reproduction and Sex Script for Preschoolers

"We need to talk"

Here's what a conversation with a five-year-old about reproduction might sound like.

HIM: Where do babies come from?

YOU: Why do you want to know?

This is a good and useful question. It will clearly help you approach your answer with some sensitivity and understanding if you know the context and source of his question. You can then use that information to shape your answer so he can better understand it.

HIM: I just do. Max said his mom is going to have a baby. She's fat and says the baby is inside her.

Now you know the context and can better answer his question by relating it to what he's seen and heard: his friend's mom is obviously pregnant and your son is interested in the why and how of it.

YOU: Yes, that's right. Babies grow inside their mom's tummy.

HIM: How does it get there?

Handle this one in a clear, clinical way.

YOU: Moms and dads make babies together and they grow inside the mom's tummy.

HIM: How?

YOU: It's a pretty simple and beautiful thing. Men have little seeds called sperm, and women have eggs. When a man and a woman love each other, they become even closer by having sexual intercourse. This may sound funny to you and you may even want to say something like "Oh! yucky," but when a mom and a dad have sexual intercourse, the daddy puts his penis into the mommy's vagina. He moves it about and eventually his penis squirts little things called sperm into the vagina. If any of the sperm reaches the mom's egg inside her tummy, it begins to make a baby. The baby grows inside the mommy, and after nine months, it gets born through the vagina.

You can be quite detailed in your explanation. This is actually much easier for you to do with young children than with older ones who have learned street talk and street "wisdom" about all kinds of things sexual.

HIM: Oh! Yucky. I'm never going to make babies.

This is not an unusual reaction, although it often comes from older rather than younger boys. Girls are much more accepting of the facts.

YOU: That's fine. You may change your mind when you get older. Do you have anything else you want to ask me?

HIM: No.

He's young and has heard enough. Now it's time for him to move on and maybe think about what you've told him. He can compare notes with his friend.

Conversations with School Children

Your ten-year-old daughter tells you she has a crush on a boy in her class and wants to know how to make him like her. You remember that when you were her age, you were so crazy about this one boy you would have done anything to get him to notice you. Can you tell this to your daughter?

You certainly can. The fact that your daughter easily confides in you indicates you have a good relationship, one where you have shared much in the past and now you can continue to share. Girls and boys start noticing and talking about liking someone of the opposite sex as early as age five or six. But it's not until age nine or ten that girls and boys really start getting "interested" in each other. They pay special attention to the object of their affections without knowing why.

Sexual play begins in earnest as boys chase and tease girls and girls run away and shriek. Girls flock together and talk about who is cute and who isn't. This is a good time to talk about specific aspects of sex with your child. Not about reproduction or the other physical aspects of a sexual relationship, but about courtesy, respect, and responsibility that goes into any relationship. Talk about the obligations they have toward someone they have a crush on. Boys and girls need to learn how to think and talk in a realistic, wholesome, and positive way toward those they really like. It's great to do this before the adolescent hormones take over completely and everything runs wild in junior and senior high school.

Discussing Young Boy/Girl Relationships

Talking about your child's feelings toward someone establishes a foundation for understanding the meaning of their feelings. Go beyond that by seeing how your child behaves toward the other child. For example, see who he gives a card to on Valentine's Day, and see who gives him one. You and your child can organize a party at your house for his friends. Observe how they interact with each other. This will give you great insight into their relationships.

Here are some great topics for talk about young boy/girl relationships:

- Thoughtfulness—we must think positively about another person.

- Respect—we need to consider other's rights, not just our own.
- Consideration—think about what others want and need before you think about what you want and need.
- Empathy—always try to put yourself in the other person's place.
- Appreciation of differences—boys and girls are different, and boys are different from each other, and girls are different from each other. Remember the positive value of differences among individuals, regardless of gender.

Here are some good openings for talking about budding relationships:

- You really like Tommy, don't you?
- How do you feel about Mary?
- Do you have someone special you want to give a card?
- Who's your special friend in class?
- Is there one boy/girl you really like in your school?

Your child may experience the problem of unreciprocated "love." That can demand more talk than successful relationships. You need to be there to listen, console, advise (when asked), and put things into perspective as much as that's ever possible in these kinds of situations, even with preadolescent children. Here are some good ways to begin conversations about this:

- Are you feeling sad?
- Did something happen in school today that you didn't like?
- Can you tell me about her/him? Did she/he do something or say something that makes you unhappy?

Once you get your daughter talking, you can start to probe a little about how she will cope with this kind of disappointment, and you can offer advice:

- Tell me what you're feeling. Are you angry, sad, or do you feel something else.
- It's okay to feel the way you do. When we don't get what we want it can make us sad.
- Let's go for a walk and talk about things. We can go to the playground and you can have some fun while we chat.
- I find that when I'm unhappy, I like to draw pictures/write things down/make lists of things that make me feel happy. Would you like to do that?
- Is there anything I can do to make you feel better?
- I'm always here for you. You can tell me anything you want and I'll listen and try to make you feel better.

It's wrong to minimize, dismiss, or ignore feelings of happiness or sadness your child might have in any boy/girl relationship. Your child may be young, but his feelings are real. These are important matters and an important stage in his social and emotional development. They matter very much to your child and to his feelings of self-esteem and belonging. They matter at school and they matter outside of school, within your child's group of friends. You know that time will heal any wounds that may occur, but you should also remember your own early "love" and "rejection," and how it made you feel.

The most important lessons on sexuality for children at this age come from parents. It's wonderful if you can give your child the support, confidence, and conversation on how best to accept and thrive on strong feelings of affection, even love, for another child. Your openness to and acceptance and recognition of your child's real and legitimate feelings, shown in your conversations, is an important part of her growing up to be a healthy, loving, and caring person.

The Reproduction and Sex Script for School Children

"We need to talk"

You're not going to talk about reproduction with your school-age children. They should know the facts of life, in a rudimentary way, by the time they're nine or ten because you talked to them about it when they were preschoolers, or they learned about it in school. You're going to have a chat about something even more important and real to them at this age: caring, affectionate relationships, and having a crush.

> **YOU:** So you have a crush on a boy at school. I think that's wonderful. What's his name?

Your initial reaction will set the tone for the rest of the conversation. If you're negative you daughter won't tell you much now, and maybe, ever. So set this up for a full and open talk by being positive and encouraging.

> **HER:** His name is Dylan.
>
> **YOU:** Tell me about him.

Ask a very open-ended question, leaving it up to your daughter to tell you what she thinks is important.

> **HER:** He's really nice. He's as tall as I am. Dark brown hair. I like his smile.
>
> **YOU:** You really like him? Why?

You want to know what attracts your daughter to boys in general and this boy in particular.

> **HER:** I don't know. I just do. And I really want him to like me. I'd just die if he didn't.
>
> **YOU:** Does he like you?

This is a very direct, tough question, but worth asking to prepare you for anything that you might have to say or do in the future.

> **HER:** I think so. He told Reagan that he likes me.
>
> **YOU:** Does he know you like him? Did you tell him?

This will tell you how your daughter operates. You hope she didn't tell him, that she's shy enough not to have done that.

> **HER:** I think so. I think Reagan told him. I'd do anything for him to like me.
>
> **YOU:** I hope you don't mean that. It's great for you to like him, but nothing you do can make him like you. He either likes you the way you are or he doesn't.

This is a bit harsh, but necessary. The earlier she learns this, the better. You don't want her to try to do things to please boys—that could be real trouble.

> **HER:** But I want him to like me so much.

She's really smitten, even though she's ten years old. It's real, and you have to help her handle the feeling. You need her to trust you now more than ever.

> **YOU:** If he's as nice as you think, he will like you for who you are. You don't have to do anything special. Please trust me on this.

The message is "Be yourself." Encourage the kind of self-esteem that every girl and woman should have in order to enjoy healthy relationships with boys and men.

HER: But I'll just die if he doesn't.

YOU: You won't die. But why worry about it now? You still don't know whether he knows you like him and whether he likes you. When you find out, let's talk some more. Until then, just be yourself. You're a lovely little girl, not a chameleon. You can't change yourself to be what you think a boy wants. The most important thing is that boys like you for yourself, who you really are.

This is the message you have to send over and over while she's developing from a little girl into a young lady. Emphasize how important it is for her always to be herself. It's obvious to us, but not to a ten-year-old with a crush.

HER: Okay, I'll try, but it won't be easy.

YOU: I'm always here to help you. I love you.

Young schoolgirls get bombarded with conflicting messages about who they are and who they're supposed to be. Even at this age, sexuality begins to be an issue for these girls and some can handle it better than others, if they even recognize it. No matter what a girl's background and upbringing, she will benefit from parents' constant support and reinforcement of her intrinsic worth.

Conversations with Teens

Your fifteen-year-old daughter tells you she wants to start taking birth control pills. You think, "She's so young, what have I done wrong? Is my teenage daughter sleeping around? Do I want to encourage this? Is it better to be safe than sorry? I don't know what to do, what to say."

Hormones kick in and puberty and adolescence come earlier to some children and later to others. For you, adolescence brings out your worst fears about the possibility of sex between consenting,

exploring teens. It conjures up visions of AIDS, other sexually trans-
mitted diseases, pregnancies, and wanton, lewd, and other immoral
behavior. Adolescence is a time when many parents want to send
their girls to a convent school to protect them from the raging hormones in boys. How can you ensure boys and girls control these
urges? What can a parent say that will promote healthy feelings, prevent promiscuity, and encourage normal sexuality?

No need to worry if you've done your job; this is when all the
early work you did pays off. Your son knows about the physical
aspects of sex and has some experience of the emotions involved.
He knows about the vagina, penis, intercourse, menstruation, mas-
turbation, and virginity. He knows about other sexual practices,
maybe not from you (there is limit on what kinds of sexual behavior
even the most enlightened and liberal parents are comfortable talking about with their son or daughter), but certainly from friends
and other sources.

Now that the physical side is a very real possibility and the emotional side can be stronger than ever, you have the opportunity and
obligation to help your teen control himself. It's time to talk seriously about what's acceptable and unacceptable behavior. Here are
some ways to start the conversation:

- I know we've talked about sex ever since you were small, but we
  need to talk about it again. Are you okay with that?
- Before you find yourself in a serious relationship, even though
  you're entirely too young to even think about it, I think we
  should talk about what's going on out there and what you think
  about teens' sexual behavior we hear and read about?
- We talked a lot about sex as you were growing up. Now I think
  we need to talk more about you and your relationships. I have

to know what you think about sex before marriage and you need to know what I think.

- I know you know all about sex. I think we need to talk about the things that should go along with sex, and which I think are sometimes missing. Things like dangers, consequences, respect, love, responsibility, right, and wrong.
- We all have to live with rules, some of which we agree with and some we don't. Can we talk about rules about sex? I think it's important we do so that I understand your views and you understand mine.

Who Can Your Teen Talk to about Sex?

When your teen wants or needs to talk about sexual issues can she talk to you? Will she talk to you? It's important that you know because she needs an adult to talk to, and if not you, then who?

For some, the family doctor or clergyman would be the answer. Or it could be a relative or close family friend. It's important for you to talk to your teen about whom he can confide in if he feels it's something he can't talk to you about.

Here are some good ways to talk about this:

- I know there are some things you don't think you can talk to me about. Who do you think would be the best person to talk to?
- I will listen to anything you need to talk about, including sex. I will not judge you or overreact. But if there's something you'd rather talk to someone else about, what about _____? Would you like to talk to him/her?
- Let's make a list of people you'd feel comfortable talking to about any sexual issues that might come up in case I wasn't around to listen or you'd rather not talk to me about them.

This kind of talk gives your teen some options that even the closest, most open family might need at times.

Safety and Values

You've spent lots of time as your children have grown talking to them about important matters, including sex. But you recognize that you can't control your teen's life and that sometimes circumstances arise which neither you nor she had planned for, and things could happen which could have serious consequences. You want to be realistic and give your child the information and protection she needs so the undesirable consequences of sex, should it happen, are minimal. This means talking about safe sex. Here are some good conversations to have:

- Talk about values, respect for the other person, and their responsibility to that person and themselves.
- Talk about the importance and use of contraceptives.
- Talk about doing the right thing.

First, talk about appropriate sexual behavior, getting their views, and giving them yours. Don't preach; be conversational and low-key even though the topic is crucial. Here are some good openings:

- I think it's time to share some thoughts related to sex. I'd love to hear what you think about sex before marriage. But first, let's agree on what we mean by sex.
- What do you think makes it okay to have sex with someone? I'd really like to know your thoughts on that. And then I'll share mine with you.

- I think sex is partly about love and excitement, and partly about values and our respect and responsibility to the other person. What do you think about that?
- I need to know how much you know about protection when people have sex. I'm not in any way encouraging you, but you're your own person and you need to know this stuff for your sake and mine. Do you think that's a realistic thing to say?
- I don't think vaginal penetration, oral sex, or any other kind of exchange of body fluids is a good idea at your age, but I'm a realist and think you need to know all the ways to protect yourself and your partner if the situation ever arises. Do you agree?
- Unprotected sex is probably the worst mistake a teen can make. I want you to promise me that you will never do that. Of course, I'd like you to promise me you won't have sex at all until you're older, but first things first. Does that make sense? Are you all right with that?

A major component of your discussion about sex and your child's behavior has to do with trust between the two of you. Consider these openings to the conversation that touch on the issue of trust:

- I've always felt you and I could talk freely about anything, sex included, and I think we both feel that way now. I think you are a fine person who has good values and cherishes and respects relationships. I know I can trust you to do the right thing, and you and I agree pretty much on what that is in most situations. What do you think?
- I think we need to talk about sex before marriage. There are different views on this and I would like to know what you think.

I know you and think you will be sensible and respectful of yourself in every situation.
- What do you think about religious beliefs that say that sex out of wedlock is a sin? Do you agree with this idea or do you have a different point of view? I would like to hear what you think.

What Not to Say When Talking to Your Kids about Sex

You can probably give examples of what not to say about sex as well as I can, but here are a few phrases I would strongly urge you to avoid:

- You're much too young to know those words.
- Don't ever say that word again.
- Sex is evil and dirty.
- If I ever hear you talk about sex again, I'll wash your mouth out with soap.
- What would our friends think if they knew?
- We don't talk about that in our house.
- How can you look at those pictures/magazines/movies/videos? They're all about sex, and sex is wrong.

It's extremely important for you to talk about sex with your kids from the earliest possible age so they are well prepared as anyone can be to cope with the demands of their sexuality. It may be hard for you to do this in the beginning, but the earlier you start the easier it will be as they grow up.

Remember, talking to your child about sex in an honest way, at whatever age he starts to ask about it, and even before, can only help him grow up loving and responsible. Once you've done that, there's not much more you can do. Now it's up to him.

The Reproduction and Sex Script for Teens

"We need to talk"

At the beginning of this section, you read a possible scenario including your fifteen-year-old daughter telling you she wants to start taking birth control pills. This is a tough topic of conversation, and one you might find yourself dealing with one day. Here's a possible scenario:

> **HER:** I want to get a prescription for the pill.
>
> **YOU:** Are you joking? You're only fifteen years old. You're far too young to be having sex.

This is a calm reaction to your daughter's statement.

> **HER:** Don't be silly, lots of girls my age are on the pill—just in case. I'm not saying I'm having sex now, but you never know.

She's probably right. Lots of teens can get a prescription, even without their parents knowing. Many would say that's a good thing because it can prevent unwanted pregnancies. Many others would say it simply encourages young girls to have sex long before they should.

> **YOU:** You're probably right. I'm sure a lot of girls your age smoke as well, but that doesn't mean it's a good thing. My concern is that I think you're too young to be having sex and I think taking the pill will encourage you to do it. We've always been honest with each other and I'm not going to stop being honest now. I don't think you should have sex until you're in a solid loving relationship with someone. Do you love a boy?

This is a bit risky because fifteen-year-olds can really be in love. Now the question is where do you go from here?

> **HER:** Not exactly.

YOU: Have you had sex?

There's no point in playing games. Get to the point.

HER: No, and that's the truth.

YOU: Do you think you should have sex with someone just for fun?

It's good to get her to start thinking out loud about the real issues.

HER: No.

YOU: What about the risk of STDs and AIDS? Do you think having sex is worth the chance of getting something like that?

HER: I know about safe sex.

YOU: I'm glad you do, but I still think there's a risk, especially at your age. You may think you're mature and sensible, but boys your age may not be.

The safe-sex problem needs mentioning because it takes two people to be safe and teens can be risk takers. It's a good idea to get her thinking about these things even if she has done so before.

HER: I want your permission to go on the pill. You know I can get it even without you.

YOU: I know, and I'm really pleased you asked me first. I'll tell you what I think and you can tell me what you think.

There's no point in temporizing. Say what you think is important and see if some reasonable compromise can be reached. Unless you're prepared to lock your daughter away, you have to be realistic.

HER: Okay.

YOU: The bottom line is this: It's bad for you to have sex at your age. Bad for you, bad for the boy, bad for the parents. All sorts of bad things can happen, and nothing good, all for a few seconds of pleasure. It can hurt your health, your reputation, and your feelings. You're fifteen. I'm willing to go along with the pill for you, but not this year. I want you to wait until you're seventeen and then talk to me about it again. And I need you to promise me you won't have sex until we talk again. Two years seems a very long time I know, but really, it isn't.

There's a method in your madness. You don't expect her to be willing to wait two years, but if she even comes back with one you're at least ahead by a year.

HER: Two years is crazy, but I'd be willing to wait until I'm sixteen.

YOU: Okay, I can live with that. In a year, we'll talk again, but in the meantime, no sexual intercourse.

You specify sexual intercourse because that's the real danger. Other things may happen, but you have even less authority over that kind of sexual behavior.

This is probably the best outcome you can hope for given the actual degree of control you have over the situation. You must hope that you have developed a relationship of trust and respect with your teen that will make her keep this bargain.

"We need to talk"

Chapter 2

Conversations about Right and Wrong

ONE DAY I passed two moms with their preschoolers ambling along beside them. One of the kids had obviously just taken a toy from another and his mom was urging him to do the right thing and give the toy back to the other child. He actually returned the toy, and the mom said a very forceful, "Good boy!"

Parents spend a great deal of time praising, blaming, and labeling their children's behavior as right or wrong, good or bad. It's what parents do, and what they are supposed to do. Otherwise, how would kids become good, responsible, mature adults?

Of course, it doesn't stop once we grow up. We are always our parents' children and they will always feel obliged to tell us what we've done right and what we've done wrong. Sometimes conversations with kids about right and wrong go well and sometimes not so well.

People are self-centered creatures, and preschoolers are notoriously so. They see a toy they want, and they grab it. They want to go down the slide, and they push others out of their way. They don't yet understand the idea of right and wrong, because their world is still very simple. They're only just beginning to form relationships with other children and understand the consequences of their behaviors and actions.

The ideals of right and wrong teach us humility. They remind us that we are not gods, and the world was not made to satisfy all our selfish desires. They remind us what may be good for us may not be good for others. That's where the idea of right and wrong begin to make sense for us and for our children. When we say, "Good girl" or "Bad boy" we are not speaking for ourselves, but for a larger, universal truth about the world. Namely, notions of right and wrong go beyond our likes and dislikes and speak to universal truths about our behavior and our relationships with ourselves and others.

Right and wrong belong to what the German philosopher Immanuel Kant called the categorical imperative. He meant that when we make decisions based on what we think is right or wrong, we are actually making those decisions for everybody for all time, not just for ourselves in that moment. The Ten Commandments exemplify this idea. So do most of our views about our children's behavior. When we say, "That was a wonderful thing to do" or "Cheating on a test is wrong," we are telling our children this is the right or wrong way to behave, not just now, but always.

While self-centeredness can be negative when taken to the extreme, we also need to see the value of self-centeredness. While we recognize the danger of our unquenchable need for self-gratification, we must also recognize why we need our ego and its drives within us. We need to look out for ourselves because we can never be sure that others will do it for us—they may be just as involved in looking out for themselves.

Here's where the ideals of right and wrong again give our lives strength. They protect us from overweening egotism. We give our children a wonderful and precious gift by teaching them right and wrong because through these conversations we teach them how to appreciate and respect the needs of others, while still appreciating their own.

We owe it to our children to talk about right and wrong even when we don't have all the answers; in fact, precisely because we don't have all the answers. We don't need to have all the answers. By talking to them about uncertainties regarding right and wrong, we show them how to approach questions of, "Did I do the right thing?" and "What's the right thing to do?" As adults and parents, we know we're always asking ourselves these questions; it makes sense to explore the same kinds of questions with our children.

Thinking about right and wrong as examples of different kinds of law can help get these concepts across. Harold Berman, a great legal scholar who taught at Harvard Law School, said when a child says, "It's my toy," that's property law. When a child says, "You promised me," that's contract law. When a child says, "He hit me first," that's criminal law. And when a child says, "Daddy said I could," that's constitutional law.

Keep these distinctions in mind as you explore the rights and wrongs of everyday life with your children. They will help you make sense of them for yourself and your child.

Conversations with Preschoolers

Let's say your son is very aggressive toward other children when he's playing with them. He takes their toys, won't share his, pushes them out of the way, and constantly bosses other children around, regardless of their age, size, or gender. You're at your wit's end, not knowing what to do or how to do it. You're afraid the other children and their parents will reject your boy and he will end up with nobody who will play with him. Furthermore, he's supposed to start kindergarten next year, and his behavior won't endear him to the teacher or the other children. You need to teach him some lessons about right and wrong behavior.

I know a child who was very much like this, and it made his parents constantly worry. What could they do to stop this antisocial behavior? They asked various experts and got some good advice that they applied to their son, and were very successful. His aggression toward others changed into playing with them in acceptable ways. He stopped grabbing, pushing, taking, and bossing. Their approach involved recognizing the reasons some children behave as he did and using that knowledge to help him change. It recognized that preschool children can learn they have choices to make and parents are there to help them recognize that, as well as point out that actions have consequences. By helping children recognize the likely consequences of their actions, we can help them choose the right behavior.

Preschool children make most of their decisions by looking at the direct consequences of their actions. They want a toy that some other child has, so they simply take it. That makes sense to them; but they also want to avoid punishment, so if taking that toy results in them having to return the toy and being removed from the play group, it may begin to make sense to them that taking someone's toy may satisfy one desire but not some others. If you consistently act to make sure your child experiences undesired results from her actions, she will begin to make the connections.

Children at this age understand direct consequences better than abstract moral reasoning. Reward and punishment may seem a simplistic way to approach right and wrong, but at this age, children understand and respond to it fairly well. It would be silly for you to go into a long explanation of why some actions are right and some wrong when the child is not thinking at that level. Connecting it to concrete examples with concrete actions and consequences helps them understand.

You want to help your child develop the skill of reasoning about right and wrong actions, starting a rudimentary set of ethical ideas and principles such as hurting others is wrong, helping them is right, taking what belongs to someone is wrong, sharing is right. You do this by labeling their behavior as right or wrong in very explicit language in a specific situation.

- Sharing your toy with Lizzie was the right thing to do.
- It's wrong to take Peter's toy.
- Good boy for taking turns.
- Pushing ahead is the wrong way to behave.

The Right and Wrong Conversation Script for Preschoolers

"We need to talk"

The aim is not for you to control your child, but to help him understand that self-control can result in greater happiness, helping him see the big picture, to overcome the egotistical urge present in all of us for the sake of a larger good for himself and others.

The following is a sample conversation you might have with your son, the little boy who takes, pushes, bosses, and doesn't share with other kids.

YOU: We need to talk.

Talk to him away from the play situation so you have a chance of getting his full attention.

HIM: But I want to play.

YOU: That's what we need to talk about—you don't know how to play.

He won't understand this until you start giving him concrete examples. Even then, it will take time for this message to work. It's not a one-shot thing.

HIM: I do.

He believes he does.

YOU: You think you do, but you're making the other children angry with you. Soon they won't want to play with you because you push them away, you take their toys, you boss them around, and you don't share. Is that what you want to happen?

You need to start right away by explaining how his actions will have consequences. He knows anger and he knows playing. He also knows sharing, pushing, and bossing around.

HIM: But they play with me.

He's right, but he isn't able to foresee the consequences of his behavior toward them.

YOU: They may be playing with you today, or even tomorrow, but they will stop playing with you if you keep doing things that make them angry with you.

Keep reminding him of the consequences. These are important things for him.

HIM: I don't make them angry.

He doesn't see or he does see but he doesn't care. He's still young enough not to see the long-term consequences of his actions. You must emphasize them.

YOU: Yes you do. Do they have happy faces when you take the toy they're playing with? Do they like it when you push ahead of them and knock them over? Do they smile at you when you don't share your toys with them?

The more explicit images you can use the better. You can even get him in conversation with his friends and ask them to tell him how they feel when he takes a toy away from them.

HIM: I don't know.

YOU: Well, they don't. You have to learn to play with your friends the right way, not the wrong way.

Now you need to put right and wrong into a concrete context that he will understand.

HIM: What's that?

If he asks you to explain this idea, that's a big plus in this conversation. Remember to do it in terms he'll connect with.

YOU: You must not take toys your friends are playing with without their permission. You must not push them over if they are ahead of you. You must not yell at them and tell them what to do. And you must share your toys with them.

You can't be much more explicit than this unless you can refer to immediate past behavior with a specific child.

HIM: But they don't share with me.

He probably believes this. His idea of sharing and yours can be very different.

YOU: That's because you don't share with them. If you do, they will, too. Sharing means letting your friends play with your toys when they want to, not just when you want to let them.

You know I love you very much, that's why I want you to know the right thing to do and to do it. Then your friends will really want to play with you. If you don't, then they won't want to play with you anymore.

Will you try? I'll help you, and I'll ask your friends to help you, too. I'll tell you when you're doing things right and when you're doing things wrong.

The rest is up to you and him. Remove him from play when he does things wrong and explain what he's done and why you've taken him away. Tell him the right thing to do, and tell him when he gets it right.

Conversations with School Children

At this age, roughly nine, ten, or eleven, your child has a fairly good sense of justice and fair play, of right and wrong. Their school experience with friends, classmates, and teachers will have helped them know right from wrong, but also to know that sometimes they have to do the wrong thing for what they may think is the right reason.

For example, they know you want them to do well in school, so they dread bringing home a report card that doesn't live up to your expectations. This may lead them to cheat on assignments or tests.

Or maybe your child is suffering from what she perceives is a great wrong done to her by a friend or classmate, teacher, or adult other than you. You need to have a conversation about right and wrong when a child thinks she's right and a grownup thinks she's wrong. Society has pretty strong beliefs about what children should and should not do, what they should and should not expect from adults, and what their rights and privileges are. Children often disagree with these beliefs; adults see children as wrong because they don't recognize children's perceptions of their own rights.

At this age, you can talk about the intentions of actions as well as their consequences. When you start talking about intentions, right or wrong becomes much more complicated than it was with preschoolers, because your child can probably justify his actions as the result of good intentions, even if the consequences are bad.

Gender presents another complicating feature for the right and wrong conversation at this age and older. As I wrote in an earlier book, "Biology seems to work against boys being as good as girls. Girls seem less naturally aggressive and better at empathizing with others and developing and valuing relationships." Your conversations about right and wrong with your daughter will be different from those with your son. Girls are generally better at obeying rules and social conventions, giving more stability to relationships inside and outside the family. They seem to see value in living up to what they believe is their perceived role in society.

Boys, on the other hand, are very good at getting into trouble, especially at school. It may not be their fault, of course. Nevertheless, more young boys than girls say school is boring, they don't read as well or as much, they don't write as well or as much, they are more likely to be suspended, and they are four times more likely to be diagnosed with ADHD in their early school years. They are more aggressive, more physical, more violent, more risk taking, and more unruly.

Girls are better at conversations about right and wrong, but boys need them more. Girls verbalize their feelings more easily, which means you need to help your boys do it. Boys have serious thoughts about right or wrong, but may need your urging to say them out loud. Your conversations with your son can help him learn how.

Your daughter needs good conversations about right and wrong in her life that may be troubling you or her. Girls can keep hurts or fears about doing the right or wrong thing bottled up, and your job is to take the lid off so they can be expressed.

Creating the kind of relationships with your daughter and son where they can talk about anything without fear of the consequences takes years. Hopefully, you've built a relationship based on trust, honesty, openness, and unconditional love. That will make talking about right and wrong in any circumstance that much easier.

The Right and Wrong Conversation Script for School Children

"We need to talk"

"That's not fair," your nine-year-old son said one evening after dinner. He was giving vent to his feelings about you letting his six-year-old brother get away with not doing his chores on Saturday. This is true—you didn't punish him, because he's generally a good boy and you were feeling lazy, it was Saturday. Now you have to defend your decision and make it seem like you did the right thing for the right reason. What can you say?

HIM: Robbie didn't do his chores and you didn't do anything. When I miss mine, you ground me. It's not fair. It's not right.

He is right about that.

YOU: You're right, it wasn't fair, and I'm sorry.

This is a good beginning. It almost never hurts to admit you're wrong when you have been. It clears the air and lets you get on with the important part of the conversation—what to do about it.

HIM: Next time I don't do mine you won't do anything to me, right?

This seems fair to him.

47

YOU: Wrong. You have to do yours and he has to do his. Next time I won't let it pass.

This is a misstep for you. You are committing yourself to a course of action that doesn't give you any wiggle room and you haven't really thought things through. You're talking from a set of abstract principles here, rather than thinking about you, your children, and your relationship with them.

HIM: Why did you do nothing this time?

A good question.

YOU: I was wrong not to have done something. We all have a contract with each other, an agreement that makes our family work. Robbie broke his part of the agreement and I should have told him he was wrong and given him a penalty. But I didn't, because he's usually very good about doing his jobs.

This is both good and bad. Using the contract analogy may need a bit more explaining for a nine year old to understand, but once he understands it, it can work for you. But your justification is weak, especially in light of what you said earlier.

HIM: So am I.

He has a point!

YOU: You're right, and I was wrong. There should have been consequences for his actions and there weren't. So what should I do? Should I punish Robbie?

Asking your child for advice on how to right a wrong is always a good move. They have a highly developed sense of fairness by this age and you should listen to it very carefully.

HIM: Maybe. But maybe you should excuse me from my chores next Saturday.

This is a fair request.

YOU: Okay, I think that's fair. That would be the right thing to do. Robbie was wrong not to do his jobs and I was wrong not to punish him for that, so I think it would be wrong not to treat you the same as I treated him.

Right and wrong aren't always clear in the moment, but when you have a chance to think about what happened, it's often much easier to see what was wrong and to try to put it right.

In this case, your son did the first wrong by not doing his chores. You did the second by not calling him to account for that. Now you can put it right by giving your other son a privilege you've already given his brother.

Conversations with Teens

Teens can think abstractly quite effectively, reason logically, and draw conclusions from the information available to them. They know, abstractly, vicariously, or from direct experience, what it means to love another person. They can see shades of gray in behavior, even if they choose to ignore them on issues of right and wrong that directly affect them. They can understand and provide logical arguments justifying their own values and behavior and condemning others.

In other words, teens have the intellectual tools for adult thinking and behavior. What they lack is the practical experience of the world in which they are responsible for others as well as themselves. Teens are supremely self-centered, self-important, and self-righteous. They want all the rights and privileges of adulthood, but they don't really want the responsibilities. Any conversations about right and wrong need to take all these teenage traits into account, even if your teen doesn't exactly fit the stereotype.

Once you throw responsibilities into the mix of right and wrong, the world becomes a much less black and white, right and wrong kind of place, and shades of gray dominate the landscape. Teens already have a good sense of right and wrong in the world at large, sometimes in agreement with and sometimes at odds with your own beliefs. You want to focus on how they act, what they say, and what they do according to their own rules of right and wrong. With your help and guidance, you want them to stay out of trouble—not out of fear of punishment, but from a good sense of right and wrong.

This sense of right and wrong for teens can come from your religious beliefs or your own ethical teachings, regardless of their source. The conversations you want to have with your teen can be wide ranging, and any talk about ethical issues at any level is all for the good; it builds your relationship through the exchange of views, ideas, and arguments. But the most important conversation you can have puts personal behavior toward oneself and others front and center.

The Right and Wrong Conversation Script for Teens

"We need to talk"

We can find a great deal to talk to teens about by using the ideas from a branch of philosophy called virtue ethics. Virtue ethics approaches questions of right and wrong by asking questions about what qualities and virtues make a "good" life. It asks how a morally good person would act in any situation. It makes for an interesting conversation with your teen, whether she seems a person who understands right and wrong actions or not.

If your teen tends toward trouble, this conversation becomes even more important as a window into their mind, beliefs, and motivations. Of course, such teens may not want to talk to you, but, if you can start such a conversation with them, you'll find it rewarding as long as you keep your cool and refrain from judging. Here's an example of what such a conversation may sound like and how you can manage it. It's just a beginning, and necessarily incomplete. But you will see how it could lead to many more interesting, revealing, instructive conversations.

YOU: I have a problem that I'd like you to help me solve.

Starting with the focus on you reduces threat levels for your teen. Asking your teen to help you creates a feeling of cooperation and a legitimate reason for conversation.

HIM: What?

YOU: I saw something today and I think I was totally wrong in what I did, but I'm not sure.

This story, whether true or not, raises an ethical dilemma that virtually everyone will face at one time or another, namely, what are my responsibilities to other people, even those I've never met?

HIM: What did you do?

You've got his interest and he's willing to listen.

YOU: I was in the parking lot at the store and I saw this woman back out of her parking spot and scratch the side of another car.

It's a realistic example and could happen to anyone.

HIM: What's wrong with that?

This question indicates a possible ethical gap in your child's thinking.

YOU: I didn't do anything.

True or false, it creates the issue of right and wrong that needs discussing.

HIM: What could you do? You didn't scratch someone's car.

This gives you the opening you need to start asking questions about right and wrong behavior.

YOU: That's what I wanted you to help me with. Should I have stopped the woman and told her to leave a note on the car she scratched? Should I have taken her license plate number and left a note on the other car myself? Should I have waited 'till the person returned to their car and told them what I saw and given them the license number?

These are the relevant issues spelled out.

HIM: I don't know. Why ask me?

A typical teen response. It's got nothing to do with him because it's someone else's actions. It shows almost no ability to empathize and little ethical thought.

YOU: Have you never seen someone do something wrong?

This question must be asked, because it redirects the problem to the teen's experience.

HIM: Sure, lots of times; everyday at school. Kids cheat, lie, and steal.

Your teen can say this unselfconsciously as though he was describing what happened in a movie.

YOU: And you do nothing?

Your teen might never have thought to ask himself this question.

HIM: What am I supposed to do—snitch on my friends?

This exemplifies the gang mentality.

YOU: What about right and wrong?

Your teen hears this as a strange question.

HIM: What about it?

Perhaps he thought about right and wrong for a moment, but it didn't seem an issue.

YOU: Don't you think it's wrong to steal, lie, and cheat?

A good general question about specific actions that gets to the heart of your concerns.

HIM: Yes. Maybe. It depends.

Your teen enters the realm of situation ethics—right and wrong depend on the situation.

YOU: Depends on what?

You need to go deeper by asking for clarification.

HIM: Who's doing it.

Right and wrong actions are tied to the people, not the principle.

YOU: Why should that matter?

Get him to reflect on what he's saying.

HIM: If it's a friend of mine doing it, I wouldn't do anything. If someone's doing it to my friend, I'd try to stop them.

If the person is a member of my gang it's okay, if not then it's not okay.

YOU: Isn't cheating, lying, or stealing always wrong?

You're asking him to generalize, to look at the principles behind our notions of right and wrong.

HIM: No. If I'm cheating a cheat, it's okay. If I'm lying to protect a friend, it's okay. If I'm stealing to give something to someone who doesn't have anything, it's okay.

His answer makes some sense in situation ethics, but are those the values you want your son to hold?

YOU: So right and wrong always depend on the situation? Who's doing what to whom and why?

You're giving him the gist of his argument.

HIM: Yes.

It works for him.

YOU: Do you think that's the way good people should think and behave?

A legitimate question that will make his principles explicit.

HIM: Yes.

YOU: That's very interesting. Can we talk about this some more? I'd like to get your views on what good people do and what a good life is.

This conversation begins your examination of right and wrong with your teen. As such, it's a very important conversation. It gives you something to work with.

HIM: Yes, sure.

Make sure you follow this up with more conversations. But for now, you've got him thinking.

"We need to talk"

Chapter 3

Fighting and Other Aggressive Behavior

You've seen how your five-year-old always wants to be first to play with a toy, first to go down the slide, first to get a cookie, pushing other children out of the way in order to achieve her goals.

Your nine-year-old comes home with his school clothes filthy with dirt, his face bruised, and his hair disheveled. You ask what happened and he says he had a fight with another boy after school. A few minutes later, the school principal calls and asks if you would mind coming to school the next day to talk about your son's behavior toward the other children.

One day, your fifteen-year-old daughter comes home from school and you can see she's been crying. You ask what's wrong and she says she doesn't want to talk about, at least not now. The next morning she refuses to get out of bed and says she's not going to school. Again, you ask what happened and she says nothing, she just feels sick. You think you better call her school and start asking questions.

All of these little scenarios make sense to parents whose children have been too aggressive, prone to fighting, or victims of aggression and bullying. Whether your child is victim or victimizer, you can't let this pass unnoticed. Ignoring the signs of aggression, fighting, bullying, or other forms of violence will not make the problem go away. You must act!

A study of bullying among elementary school students discovered that in fifty-three episodes of bullying in the playground, in 54 percent of the cases those standing around did nothing but watch the bully picking on his victim. And in 21 percent of the cases, some of the watchers joined in. In only 25 percent of the cases did a child try to help the victim or call a teacher.

Researchers explain this behavior by pointing out that children say nothing for fear they may be next. They further suggest bullies are often very popular with the other kids, second only to students described by other children and teachers as friendly, outgoing, and self-confident. Boys known to be bullies came second in popularity, higher than perceived wimps, eggheads, and teacher's pets.

Each of the different age groups in this book have different kinds of specific issues with behavior, but they all share one thing in common—the potential for violence or actual violence. Preschoolers can push, shove, grab, take, and hit when they think they are being wronged. They can engage in a form of bullying, too. School children can fight verbally and physically, bully, and be victims of bullying. Teens bully, fight, and show very aggressive verbal behavior individually, in small groups, and in gangs.

Any kind of violent and abusive behavior needs preventive action by parents and other adults. It should never be tolerated, never have a blind eye turned in its direction, never have it said that it's a natural part of growing up, never encouraged, never ignored, pretending that if you ignore it it will go away.

Bullying is perhaps the most pervasive, insidious, and destructive of these forms of aggression, because it's the kind of violence by the bully that begets violence by the bullied, as we have seen in the Columbine shootings and other instances. The shooters were often self-described victims of bullying who were finally getting their revenge, not only on the bullies, but on the bystanders as well, the people who stood around and did nothing to prevent the bullying.

Some people justify bullying as part of growing up. Not surprisingly, victims don't see it that way. One person wrote in a letter to the *New York Times*, "…I can say that the experience [of bullying] did not help toughen me up or teach me [which behaviors to do and which to avoid]." Rather, it filled this victim with anger, shame, and resentment.

Another letter writer opined, "No matter how common bullying may be, it is a manifestation of violence and disrespect. Efforts to address it should be a priority." And a third writer joined in, saying, "The notion that bullies will be bullies, and it must ever be thus will be true only as long as there are no consequences for youth who victimize others in this way…Schools, parents and legislators must step in to stop it [bullying]. We did it for physical and sexual abuse of children. Why can't we do it for peer abuse?"

These voices of the bullied and those concerned with bullying speak eloquently of the issues of aggressive behavior and fighting parents need to talk about with their children. Your children need to know as young as possible that bullying, antisocial aggressive behavior, and violence of any kind are not allowed. It's up to you to show the way through talk and by example.

Conversations with Preschoolers

Our almost-two-year-old granddaughter hauled off and hit her one-and-a-half-year-old cousin, who had just taken a Christmas gift away from her. It's a perfect example of the kind of violence even the youngest toddlers can do. Although her behavior may seem perfectly innocent and justified under the circumstances, it's not a habit you want any child to develop. It's never too early for you to start drumming home the message that violence is a bad solution to problems, especially for children.

Hopefully, you are also the kind of person who does not use violence toward your children or others to solve your problems. If your child sees you as an aggressive (in a bad way) person, someone easily drawn to violence, you'll have a hard time convincing him you're not a hypocrite. Your words and deeds must go together.

What we ought to have done in the case of our grandchildren, but didn't, was sit down with both children and talk about the events and try to get them to tell us what was right and what was wrong. At age two, talk about fighting and aggression can still make sense because the children have experienced these things. Even if they can't articulate them, they can understand the physical acts and resulting hurt.

The Fighting and Other Aggressive Behavior Conversation Script for Preschoolers

"We need to talk"

The most important thing in this conversation, as in most conversations with children of any age, is to have them do as much of the talking as possible. Let them put the issues into their words rather than yours. Imagine that the following sample conversation is between you and your four-year-old daughter after she has had an altercation with her cousin.

YOU: Do you know why I want to talk to you?

This is to be sure that you are both talking about the same event.

HER: Yes, because I hit him.

Now you know for certain.

YOU: That's right. Do you think hitting him was the right thing to do?

Questions are a great way to begin because they let you hear your child's perspective right away and you know what you have to work on.

HER: No.

A good beginning.

YOU: Why not?

Again, you need to hear your child's reasoning before you can decide what to say next.

HER: Because it's not nice to hit people.

YOU: That's right. Do you know why it's not nice?

It's good to carry this forward so you begin to talk about the specific instance and then get to more general principles, even with young children.

HER: Yes.

YOU: Why?

Getting them to talk is so much better than preaching.

HER: Because you can hurt someone.

Good answer.

> **YOU:** That's right. Is that the only reason?

The more talking they do the more you gain an insight into their thinking.

> **HER:** Yes.

This introduces what may be a maturational limit on your child's ability to generalize from the specific incident to a general rule of good behavior.

> **YOU:** Do you like someone who hits you?

It's a good ploy to make it personal.

> **HER:** No.
>
> **YOU:** Well, that's another reason, isn't it?

Again, you can try to build a set of rules, but it may not work with a child this age.

> **HER:** What?

Don't ever assume that what's clear to you is clear to your child, at any age.

> **YOU:** Your friends won't like you if you hit them.

Words they should be able to understand.

> **HER:** Oh. But what if they take my toy?

Good question.

> **YOU:** Do you think it's okay to hit them if they take your toy?

Another good question. Do you have a good answer as well?

> **HER:** Yes.

Your child has a good answer, even if it's not the one you were looking for.

YOU: Why?

Sounds like you're unsure yourself, which is okay. These questions don't always have easy answers. You can share that bit of wisdom with your child.

HER: Because they won't give it back.

This argument has its own logic.

YOU: What should you do if they take your toy and they won't give it back?

Now you begin the closing argument.

HER: Hit them until they do?

This has a certain charm, but you must reject it.

YOU: That's not a good idea. I think it would be better to tell me or Mom so we can help you.

In this case, you had better be around to take action.

HER: What if you're busy?

Your child is way ahead of you.

YOU: We'll never be too busy to help you when you need help.

Can you guarantee this? At this age, probably yes, unless they're at a play date or in preschool. In which case this reason may come back to bite you.

HER: Okay.

She trusts you.

YOU: Good. Now do you know what to do if someone takes your toy?

Now for the test question.

> **HER:** Yes.
>
> **YOU:** Will you hit them?
>
> **HER:** No. I'll come and get you or Mommy.

Good answer!

> **YOU:** That's wonderful!

End of conversation, until it happens again and you're not there to fix it.

Conversations with School Children

Once your children start school, bullying becomes the number one threat for both boys and girls. You need to keep a constant eye open for the tell-tale signs that your son or daughter is being bullied. Suddenly your son seems reluctant to go to school each day, even though he used to love going. Your daughter complains of feeling sick in the morning and she seems to have lost her appetite. Your son wakes up in the night, perhaps crying, and doesn't want to talk about school. Your daughter can't explain what happened to her new watch, and she seems to have nothing to show from her allowance.

All of these can be signs of bullying and need investigation, starting with a good conversation about the problem of bullying. Bullying is not a rare thing in schools and it's probably most parents' main worry for their children. Kids who get bullied can have psychological scars that last a lifetime. It's destructive and sometimes encourages others to join in with the bullying of your child.

Most children are reluctant to admit it, report it, and step in and try to stop others from being bullied.

Fighting among school children can erupt at any time children find themselves targets of teasing and bullying and refuse to put up with it. It's more than just a shame that these actions are allowed to get this far; in fact, it's unacceptable. More often than not, the violence, both physical and verbal, happens during school or after school on the playground or on the streets. Teachers and parents must not allow this to happen and can help by offering close supervision, or by redirecting children's energies and animosities into role playing and games where violence is controlled and students can directly experience what it's like to be a victim.

Unfortunately, schools often pay no more than lip service to concerns about bullying and other forms of violence, usually due to lack of time, money, and personnel to investigate each charge. A study by researchers at the National Institutes of Health claimed roughly 25 percent of all children of middle-school age were involved as perpetrators or victims in serious or chronic bullying that included threats, ridicule, name calling, punching, slapping, jeering, and sneering.

So you need to talk about these things with your child and make him understand you will not allow him to fight or to be bullied under any circumstances. To do this, you have to make sure you don't seem to be blaming the victim. Kids don't ask to be bullied, and often think they are powerless against it, so if your child is being bullied you don't want to add to his distress by seeming to say it's his own fault. Sometimes children must either fight or run away, and running away never seems like an acceptable option. So you need to find a way to prevent these situations from arising in the first place.

The Fighting and Other Aggressive Behavior Conversation Script for School Children

Your best options are to make sure you know your child's school has strong and well-thought-out policies against violence and bullying and that they are strictly enforced. Beyond that, you need to talk to your child about your policies and views and get your her to share her views and experiences with you. Here's what such a conversation might look like.

YOU: Hurry up. It's almost time for you to leave for school.

A standard, almost ritualistic phrase, familiar to all parents.

HER: I don't feel very well.

Another standard phrase. It can mean almost anything from real illness to a desire to stay home and play video games.

YOU: You were all right last night. What's wrong?

The probing questions must begin.

HER: My stomach hurts.

Probably not real illness, but you can't assume that.

YOU: Really? Let me have a look.

What is it, exactly, that you intend to discover by looking at your child's stomach? Of course, your child won't know that it's just a ploy.

HER: No, don't touch me. It hurts.

Ah! You're going to poke and prod.

YOU: This is the fourth time in the last few weeks you haven't felt well enough to go to school. I think we need to take you to the doctor.

Your suspicions are real and realistic because you know your child. The doctor threat is a good one. Children cannot claim illness and then refuse treatment.

HER: I don't want to go to the doctor. I'll feel better later.

The cure is on the horizon. Now you must get to the bottom of the problem.

YOU: What's wrong with school? Why don't you want to go?

You're entitled to jump ahead a few steps because you think you know where this is leading.

HER: I do. I just don't feel good.

You're right not to believe her—it's too out of character. So you state your opinion.

YOU: You're not being honest with me.

It's good for her to know you've seen right through her little game.

HER: Yes I am.

She can persist, but you'll make her realize it won't get her very far—you're too wise and all knowing.

YOU: Tell me. We've always been honest with each other. I won't be angry whatever you tell me. Just tell me the truth.

This is where the nature of your ongoing relationship really matters.

HER: Some boys are teasing me and want to hurt me if I don't give them money.

It works. She is being honest with you. You would know if she is likely to make up this kind of story.

YOU: Which boys?

A good beginning question for getting to the core of the problem.

HER: Some boys in grade eight. They wait for me at school every morning and if I don't give them some money, they poke and push me around and call me names.

YOU: This has to stop. We're going to school right now to talk to the principal.

You're absolutely right—it must be stopped right away. And the school must know about it and must help.

HER: But if I tell on them they'll really go after me.

This is a normal fear, and has some justification, but the alternative of not doing anything is worse.

YOU: No, they won't. The principal will put a stop to it and I'll be there to make sure of that.

This is not something you can guarantee, but she knows you will do your best. The rest is up to the school, the parents of the boys, and the gods.

Conversations with Teens

If you've started talking about violence and antisocial behavior with your children young enough, you might be lucky and have no problems with your teens being too aggressive or violent toward others. However, given the incompleteness of the teenage brain, and the teenage male's propensity toward risk taking, chances are you are going to have some degree of concern that your boy may get involved in fighting, bullying, or teasing others, or may be a victim.

You will also have concerns for your teenage daughter, either that she abuses others or belongs to a gang or clique that does. You don't want her to bully any more than you want her to be bullied.

The most serious effects of violence and bullying can be retaliation. Teens are old enough to know how to fight and even kill; the majority of cases of deadly school violence happen in high schools. The important indicators of potential violence, according to one expert on bullying, are victimization and how and if the teen did anything about it, school contact with parents about a serious matter that parents did nothing about, and any history of conflict or confrontation. Any of these indicators taken alone may mean nothing. However, taken together they can point to the potential for violent acts.

Furthermore, this bullying expert comes from a violent home. His mother was a heroin addict and, when he was ten years old, shot his father in front of him. He believes teen violence, like any other kind, rarely just happens. He argues that, "violence is not just an act. There are always indicators, if you know what to look for." In other words, people don't just snap—there's a history of signs leading up to the violence.

Some researchers into primate behavior claim there is an observable relationship between the bully and the bullied, such that the individuals who end up as the object of the bullying have certain characteristics, just as the bullies have. Even if it were true that some children invite bullying by their behavior, that is no reason to allow it to happen. Children who are vulnerable to teasing or even petty violence need our protection as much as children who have measles or the flu.

The Fighting and Other Aggressive Behavior Conversation Script for Teens

"We need to talk"

In this script, I want to show a conversation between a parent and son, who is a bully. I do this because if we can stop the bullies, we stop the bullying. Victims do not bully themselves.

YOU: I had a disturbing phone call from your school today.

This is a tough beginning, but a necessary one because it's the truth. You hated getting the call, but to do nothing about it would be a terrible thing for your son and for you.

HIM: About what?

YOU: About your behavior.

You can slowly let the story come out to give your son a chance to think about what's coming and how to get out of it, knowing that you won't let him escape.

HIM: What about it?

He probably already knows.

YOU: That you're bullying kids in your school.

You need to be direct, as painful as it is for you to have to say these words.

HIM: Whoever said that is a liar.

You know your son. What would you expect him to say? The question is, how well do you think you know him and how well do you really know him? What you do next is crucial.

YOU: Why would anybody say it if it weren't true?

This is a good question, logical, reasonable, and to the point.

HIM: I don't know. Maybe they've got it in for me.

He's scrambling for something to hold on to.

YOU: Who would have it in for you?

Now his imagination can go into overdrive. The list of suspects is endless.

HIM: Some of my teachers, the principal, some guys who are jealous of me.

YOU: The principal said a parent phoned her and said his son had been punched by you because he wouldn't give up his seat at the basketball game, and that you've done the same thing to him and a few other kids in the cafeteria. Is this true?

Direct confrontation means he must come up with a good story or admit that it's true, at least in part.

HIM: I never did that. I mean I didn't really punch him or the others. I just pushed them because they were in my way. They know what seat I always have at the game, and me and my friends always sit at the same table at lunch.

This is the old "what you see depends on where you're standing" ploy. You may want to accept it, but I wouldn't advise it.

YOU: This won't do. I'm making an appointment with your principal and we're both going to see her and discuss what really happened. We're going to do everything we can to make sure this kind of thing never happens again. And if it turns out that you did these things, I am going to get the phone number of the boy you punched—or pushed—and you're going to call him and apologize and promise never to do it again; not to him or anyone else. And if you give me any trouble on this, you will be grounded for more than the month I'm grounding you right now. Do you understand?

This is tough love and it's necessary. What he is accused of is unacceptable and you need to get to the bottom of it.

HIM: Aw, come on. It was nothing.

The real test will be his willingness to accept the truth and consequences of his actions and if he shows genuine contrition.

YOU: I asked if you understand.

You won't know for quite a while if he really understands his actions and their consequences and implications.

HIM: Yes, I understand.

Time will tell, but he will need your help.

YOU: If it turns out that you did what you're being accused of, we're going to sit down and you're going to tell me why you did it and how you suggest we deal with it on a long-term basis. I need your input on this because it's your behavior, not mine. We have to work together to make this kind of behavior go away for ever, for your sake and ours.

It may seem that you're prejudging the case against him before you hear all the evidence, but in a case like this, it's good to be prepared for the worst. As long as you remain calm and evenhanded, and genuinely request his input, you can only strengthen your relationship with him. This kind of behavior doesn't have a quick fix. You must work with him consistently over the long term, and seek professional help and counseling if necessary.

Chapter 4

Death of a Person or Pet

OUR CHILDREN WERE nine, ten, and twelve when our cat, Napoleon, went missing from our mountain chalet. It was a cold December night and we were getting ready for Christmas, putting up decorations inside and outside. We often let him out, even when the weather was cold and snowy, and he always returned, meowing loudly at the door.

But this night, we never heard his meow and he never returned. We searched all over that evening and the next day. Our eldest son made posters, which we put up on telephone poles in the neighborhood. We asked neighbors if they had seen him. But it was no good, and we never saw him again.

We were all heartbroken. My wife and I made up stories to ease the pain, about how he must have been picked up by a family driving by who thought he must have been lost or abandoned. Now he was enjoying their love and attention as he once did ours.

The children cried, as did we, but we also talked about what fun he was and how much we missed him. We looked at photos and talked about silly things he did, like the evening he tried jumping onto the TV and missed, then went off looking quite embarrassed about the whole thing.

Our experience of death and pets over the years is extensive, and, like most families, we have also had our share of people dying—friends, family, and schoolmates. My wife was only three when her father, a Royal Air Force flight instructor during World War II, was killed in a crash along with thirteen students. My parents adopted me as an infant. I always knew I was adopted and when, at age four or five, I asked why my "real" parents didn't want me I was told that they had died in a car accident. Our children have had their grandparents, schoolmates, and schoolmates' parents die.

Death is a huge and serious topic for people, and most of us don't want to talk about it even amongst ourselves. To talk to our children about such a normally tearful, sad occasion takes both thought and skill. As true as it is that death is a natural part of life, death that is too sudden, too close to home, too tragic, or that happens to someone or something too young doesn't seem natural at all—it seems wrong!

Wrong or right, death is a fact of life and we have to talk to our kids about it under many different circumstances. Perhaps the most important lesson you want your child to learn about the particular death you're dealing with and death in general is the importance of life. If you can help your child understand how lucky we all are to be alive, then you help her use every minute of her life wisely, doing things she values and that create value.

Conversations with Preschoolers

Preschoolers experience loss differently from older children. Their experience and knowledge of the world, as well as their cognitive ability to work with abstract ideas and concepts, limit the ways in which they understand death. They can be sad and they can grieve the disappearance of a parent, grandparent, or sibling, but their sense of someone no longer being there isn't at a conscious level, even though the memory of it may influence them later in life.

I think there must be some evolutionary advantage to this for young children, since death was a far more frequent event historically than it is today, in a society that insulates us from the experience. Death diminishes us in the sense that it places our own mortality front and center. It might also depress us and cause us to cut back on our energy and ambition, our plans for thriving in life. It might be good that very young children don't experience or understand death as we do, so that death doesn't depress them or their ambitions or confidence in life.

Given the naïveté of preschool children's understanding of death, I suggest you take a very direct, simple approach in your conversation when explaining it and the many emotions and rituals surrounding it. The thing you will probably notice is their solicitude toward you and your feelings. In your conversation, you're teaching them what to feel and how to show it.

The most interesting thing about having this conversation with young children is the degree to which the conversation is really about reassuring them you still love them even though someone or something close to you and them has died. Death is an unusual, and hopefully rare, occurrence for them, and they don't want it to threaten their relationship with you—the love and security they feel and need.

The Death of a Person or Pet
Conversation Script for Preschoolers

"We need to talk"

Our grandchildren were four and five years old when their great grandfather died. He did not suffer from a prolonged illness, so we had no time to prepare the children for his death. It took about six weeks for his health to decline from relatively good for a man his age to his death. Here's how we tackled our conversation about his death with our preschoolers. Notice that the children wanted to comfort the parent and are much more concerned about his feelings than their own.

YOU: I have some sad news kids.

It's fine for you to say right out this is sad new. It cues the children as to what their response and attitude should be.

THEM: What? What?

For young children all news is a bit exciting.

YOU: Great-grandpa died yesterday in New York. Do you remember him?

Young children don't always remember people they don't often see. If your parents live in Florida and you live in New York, your three- to five-year-old may not always have a clear memory of who they are.

HER: Yes, we saw him last summer.

The five year old will be more likely than the four year old to remember. Also, brain differences give girls better memories for these kinds of things.

YOU: That's right; I'm glad you remember him.

You can show your appreciation.

> HIM: Are you feeling sad?

Even little kids can empathize in such circumstances, mainly because they have learned to do so from watching adults do it in other circumstances or on TV or in films. They may not understand the full import of what they're saying, but they know the ritual forms.

> YOU: Yes, very sad. He was my dad.

You don't have to hide any emotions you feel, as long as you remember who you're talking to and understand that they won't appreciate the depth of your feelings intellectually, although they will viscerally understand your emotions.

> HER: Did you cry?

At this age, children are direct and want to know as much as they can about how people behave and feel.

> YOU: Yes, I did. I loved him very much.

This mention of love will give them a larger context for understanding the impact death can have on people.

> THEM: Don't be sad.

They don't want you to be sad because they think that being sad will affect your feelings and interaction with them.

> HIM: We loved him, too.

Children learn to mimic what they hear when they think it's the right thing to say, even if they don't, or can't, fully understand the meaning.

> HER: Yes, we did.

> YOU: I know you did, and I don't want you to be sad. I love you both very much.

This will comfort them. They want to be reassured in this instance that the death of their great-grandpa won't threaten your feelings for them.

HIM: I'm not sad.

HER: I'm not sad.

You asked them not be sad and they are telling you they will do as you ask because they want you to know they are good children. They want to please you because you are sad. They unconsciously realize your sadness could be a threat to your relationship with them, simply because the emotion is different and out of the ordinary.

YOU: Not at all?

You want them to be free to be sad if they want to be.

HIM: A little bit.

HER: Yes, a little bit, but we won't cry.

They want to do what you want them to do, so they will be a little sad if you want them to be. They won't go to the extreme of tears, unless they think you want them to.

YOU: I'm glad. He wouldn't want you to be sad because he loved you very much. He lived a good, long life and he had wonderful great-grandchildren like you.

You're giving them the cues to how they should feel and behave, and they'll listen to you very carefully.

HER: We're not sad.

HIM: We won't cry.

They want to reassure you they will show whatever emotions you want them to show so you'll love them.

YOU: That's good.

This reassures them.

Conversations with School Children

A little less than two weeks after the tragedy of the twin towers at the World Trade Center, The New York Times published excerpts from essays by children in grades three to six. Children in these grades would range in age from eight to eleven or twelve. This included children who attended schools only blocks from the towers and were in session as they fell. All the children escaped unharmed.

Teachers asked these children to put their feelings and thoughts on paper to better make sense of their experience. What they wrote about tells us much about how children react to sudden and violent death. In their essays and poems, they write empathetically about the fear and pain of others, about their immediate circumstances after the planes hit the towers, about the reactions of their schoolmates, and of their and others' parents who came to get them from school. Some recall running away from the dust and debris, the fears of parents for their children, and the means, manner, and whereabouts of their escape from, or isolation after, the collapse.

What's so remarkable—yet not really—is the relative selflessness of the children. They don't go on about fear of death or morbidity in the face of the horror of so many innocent deaths. They write with strong emotion and some sense of fear and astonishment, but with much more concern for others and for the country than for themselves.

Here's an example from a grade-five student:

> ### "We need to talk"
>
> "I feel so many feelings. I am thinking so many thoughts. I'm scared, relieved, but yet I feel brave and angry. What do I feel? How do I feel? Only time will tell.
>
> It's raining hard. The ground is thumping. Cool gusts of wind come through the cracks of the window. I sigh with relief."

Here's a letter that talks of death from a sixth-grade girl:

> ### "We need to talk"
>
> "When I was sitting down in class, from the corner of my eye, I saw thick gray smoke in the sky. Everybody got out of their seat and rushed to the window. I couldn't believe what I was seeing. The twin towers were on fire! It didn't hit me just then to know that so many people died. It took a couple of days to realize that it wasn't just a movie. It was really happening. I feel very upset and frustrated. I hope the victims go to heaven and their relatives try to forget this tragic moment. We should all try to live our lives to the fullest."

School children don't seem to see others' deaths as a threat to themselves in the same way adults do. They do have a certain understanding that when people die they are no longer there, but they don't really seem to feel threatened by it beyond a vague kind of fear. Children in grades five and six showed more sophistication in their writing and the way in which they conceived and understood this event, but they still did not speak overtly about their own fear of death. The way in which they wrote about death reflects a child's detachment from events in the way they don't morbidly express fears they might die, too. They wrote as observers of death rather than participants in a death-making event. Many of them also focused quickly on what to do next, rather than soul-searching for reasons, answers, and explanations for what happened around them.

Children in grades three and four took an even more abstract, yet very personal, stance. They talked about specific action in a quite unemotional way. The event out there happened at a distance, and their reactions were sincere and strong and personal, yet clearly simplistic and, for lack of a better word, disembodied. We would expect this from eight-year-olds. As they get older, their fears become a bit less generalized and more personal, but this might also be a function of their increased facility with language and self-expression.

The Death of a Person or Pet Conversation Script for School Children

"We need to talk"

Let's say your nine-year-old has a best friend whose mother just died from breast cancer. He comes to you with his concerns because his friend has been crying and telling him all about her mother's final days in a hospice. Here's an example of the conversation you might have with him.

> HIM: Samantha's mom died. I saw her at school yesterday and she couldn't talk about it without crying.

This is the opening of the problem, a bid for your attention, and reaction to this death.

> YOU: It's a hard thing, isn't it? I hope you put your arms around her and gave her a great big hug.

You want her to know that everyone needs some help and affection in the face of the death of a loved one.

> HIM: Yes, I did. I didn't know what to say, really. She was so sad. I can't imagine not having a mom. You're okay, aren't you?

It's a need for reassurance that you'll always be there.

> YOU: Yes, I'm fine. I make sure I have an examination on a regular basis. I think if anything were there, we'd catch it early enough for it to be all right.

This is the answer she needs. You're not planning to get sick and die any time soon.

> HIM: Are you sure? Sam said her mom had examinations, too, but when they found the lump it was already too late to cure it.

Even at this age, he sees that doctors and medicine are not infallible.

> YOU: That can happen sometimes, but I'm sure I'm okay.

You can only do what you can do.

> HIM: What do I do now that her mom's dead? What does she do?

Children need help with this.

> YOU: Is there going to be a funeral or a memorial service?

You need the details, and if you don't have them, you need to get them.

> HIM: I think so.
>
> YOU: Well, we'd better find out. I think it would be a good idea for you to go. I'll go with you, of course.

Your child will probably need your support here.

> HIM: Why do we need to go? I don't want to see her mom dead.

It's not an unusual question and concern from children.

> YOU: It's a good thing to go to funerals when people die, especially people you knew or loved, or people your close friends loved. It's a way to say goodbye yourself or to help your friends say goodbye. Samantha would really like you to be there, I'm sure of that.

You owe it to your child to give him a good answer. This one encourages empathy and understanding by asking your child to look beyond himself.

> HIM: But why do we have to look at dead people? It seems strange.

Your child has lots to learn about customs and rituals.

> YOU: It's just what we do. People do die and we have to help their family and friends get through the sadness. Don't you remember how we had a funeral for your little hamster? It's to help us say goodbye and get on with our lives.

It's always helpful if there's a prior experience that you can tie into.

> HIM: But what do I say to Sam? I don't know what to say or do.

YOU: The most important thing is just to be there for her when she needs someone to talk to, to listen to her, to hold her when she cries. You have to be there to show her that life goes on and that some day she will feel better.

It's good to explain that these rituals are for the living more than the dead.

HIM: You mean she'll forget about her mom dying?

This is a real and serious concern for your child.

YOU: No, she will never forget her mom. She'll always love her and think of her, but after a while, it won't seem quite so bad. She'll slowly get back to doing the things she did before with you, at school, with the rest of her family. It won't be the same, it will be different, but it won't always be so sad, even though her mom isn't there anymore.

You're right to reassure him that she'll never forget. Children need to believe their parents will always be there in one way or another.

HIM: Okay, I'll find out about the funeral. Thanks.

Conversations with Teens

When our daughter was sixteen, her boyfriend fell asleep at the wheel while driving home late and smashed into a light pole. His mother and father were in the car with him. His father was killed and he and his mother were seriously injured. He was flown by air ambulance to a nearby trauma center. Both he and his mother later recovered physically, but he was seriously injured psychologically.

All of a sudden, their lives were irrevocably changed, as was the life of our daughter. She spent much of her time at the hospital, and after, she seemed to become his therapist, as he refused to continue in counseling. He lost interest in his favorite pursuits. Some of this might also have been the result of his physical injuries.

After a year or so of this new relationship, our daughter could no longer cope with this boy's problems and the relationship ended. His father's death, the result of an accident he caused, also killed whatever had been between him and our daughter. My wife talked about it with our daughter and it became clear that the problem was with this boy's refusal to examine his feelings of guilt and remorse with professional counselors.

Teens, particularly older teens, have a good understanding of death, even if they feel invulnerable. When they experience the death of anyone close to them, they need to grieve, and sometimes they need help with this process. This has definitely been true for teens who have lost teachers and friends in school shootings or accidents.

Although violent deaths may seem to be a fact of life for today's teens thanks to media hype, it's unlikely experiencing the death of someone close is more likely now than before. That makes it even more important to talk about death with teens—to help prepare them for the death and grieving of someone they love.

The Death of a Person or Pet Conversation Script for Teens

"We need to talk"

Suppose your teen has just heard about a friend of his being killed at school. What kind of conversation would you like to have with him about the death of one of his friends, especially if he, like most teens, thinks of himself as immortal? Here's a possible script of such a conversation.

YOU: How are you feeling today? The shooting at your school was only two days ago, and I imagine you must still be a bit shocked by it all.

HIM: Yes, I am.

YOU: I never thought there could be violence like that at your school. All the kids seem to come from good homes. How could such a thing happen? And to one of your friends?

It's a concern for all parents—always has been, always will be.

HIM: Yes.

Teens are not always verbal with their parents, especially with parent-initiated conversations. Make sure your conversations are not interrogations.

YOU: When's the funeral?

HIM: Tomorrow.

YOU: You're going, aren't you?

HIM: Yes, I guess.

This sounds off handed, but is just a style of talking. Your teen doesn't want to show too much emotion. It's not cool.

YOU: How could you even think of not going? He was your close friend.

Don't get upset; just have a conversation.

HIM: Yes, I know.

YOU: How do you feel about this? A close friend dying like that?

Even a teen can give a reasonable answer to this question.

HIM: I don't know. I guess I feel bad.

Your teen may not volunteer much, but this is a beginning.

YOU: You only guess? Aren't you sure?

It will take a bit of prodding to get much out of him.

    HIM: Yes, I'm sure.

    YOU: Do you want to talk about how you really feel?

This may work, or it may not. If it doesn't, try another, more subtle, route.

    HIM: I don't know how I really feel. First, he's there and now he's gone, forever.

This teen is actually opening up a bit. You may not be so lucky.

    YOU: It's okay to feel sad. Just because you're a boy doesn't mean you can't cry when a friend dies.

You can talk about emotions, but remember that a visible display of emotion by a teenage boy is unlikely.

    HIM: I don't feel like crying.

    YOU: But you might, once this really sinks in. Do you want me to come to the funeral with you?

This is a good offer, but often refused by boys.

    HIM: No. I'll go with some friends.

    YOU: You remember when grandma died? You were really sad and cried a lot.

    HIM: I know, but I was only nine. And it was different.

Age differences are very important to teens. They are no longer children in their minds and don't want to be reminded of any of their childish behavior.

    YOU: How was it different?

It doesn't hurt to try to get your boy to think about this.

HIM: She was my grandma and I loved her, and she loved me.

He knows that this is a different kind of love than that of friend for friend.

YOU: Didn't you love your friend?

HIM: I never really thought about it.

This is probably true. But it's good that now he might think about it.

YOU: It might be a good idea for you to ask yourself how you felt about him when he was alive and how you feel about him now that he's dead. It might help you get through this.

HIM: I don't need any help.

YOU: I hear what you're saying. But if you decide you do need help, just tell me.

This might not happen now, but will be appreciated when your teen matures a bit more.

HIM: Yeah.

Don't let your son get away with this kind of inarticulateness. Prod him a bit with requests for a more open and honest expression of his feelings. Ask him how his friends are coping. Ask for details. It's more an invitation than an interrogation.

Chapter 5

Children Who Are
Different or Who Don't Fit In

YOUR CHILDREN HAVE lots of experience with other children who are different, who have some physical or mental problem, who look different, dress different, or speak a different language. Most of today's schools maintain a policy of inclusive education, which simply means children who are different are included in the "normal" classroom for most of the day, sometimes with special classes for special treatment during part of that school day.

I know that my students, who are preparing to be teachers, come back from their practice-teaching classrooms with tales of having to learn how best to help children with problems that need special care and attention. This includes immigrant children who need ESL (English as a Second Language) classes to help them learn the language of their new home. Other special classes may have teachers, psychologists, physical therapists, and medical personnel to work with children who have physical and behavioral problems that can't be addressed in the regular classroom.

Some Truisms about Us and Our Children

We're all the same and we're all different. We all fit easily into some contexts but not very well into others. We all worry about others who are different from us, for whatever reason. We don't want to have to change our habits, our customs, our ways of doing things to suit them. But we wouldn't mind them changing their ways to suit us.

We don't like the unknown, and people who look, dress, or talk differently than us are unknowns. Why can't they just fit in, we ask ourselves? But maybe we don't let them fit in even when they want to. Most peoples have a history of emphasizing differences and ignoring similarities. In some places, you will always be an "incomer" even if you arrived when you were an infant.

The first question you need to ask yourself when you raise this topic with your children is: What are my own attitudes, feelings, and behavior toward people who are different from me? Your own approach to differences will obviously color what you say to your kids, but, more importantly, your kids will have seen how you behave toward others who are different. You can't expect your children to "Do as I say, not as I do." Young children clearly learn much of their own values and attitudes from their parents. You must model the behavior you want your children to use toward people who are different, whatever those differences may be.

I believe that one of the most important goals in life is happiness. We fail as parents if we don't teach our children by word and deed how to be happy, and part of being happy is accepting the world as it comes. This doesn't mean we shouldn't try to make it better or less painful for those sick or in need, but even when faced with a world filled with pain and torment, sadness and injustice, we need to accept the fact that we live in a world where the possibility of happiness includes the possibility of unhappiness.

Denying this world because it doesn't suit our ideal version of what a world should be spills over into our relationships with others. This really is the best of all possible worlds because it is, as far as we know, the only possible world. The first three things we must teach our children about the differences they encounter in others in this world are ACCEPT, ACCEPT, ACCEPT! The second three things are TREASURE, TREASURE, TREASURE! And the last three things are LEARN, LEARN, LEARN!

Conversations with Preschoolers

There's no better time to start teaching your child to accept that people come in different genders, colors, shapes, sizes, talents, and abilities than when they begin to actually notice differences. My granddaughter started ballet lessons when she was three. Across the street from her lived a three-year-old girl who was also in her ballet class. This little girl had Down syndrome. When I went to watch my granddaughter dance, I saw that none of the other little girls in the class seemed to take the slightest interest in the fact that the girl had Down syndrome. Even though she behaved a bit differently from the other girls, often running up to her mom and dad looking, I believe, for approval and affection, none of the other girls seemed to think this the slightest bit odd or unusual. This was simply what she did.

This is as it should be, although it often isn't so. I have no way of knowing how the children talked among themselves about the girl and other children with differences, nor how they might have behaved toward them. Hopefully, their acceptance continued, although we know how intolerant and spiteful children can be toward those they perceive as not fitting in for one reason or another.

The Children Who Are Different or Who Don't Fit In Conversation Script for Preschoolers

"We need to talk"

Here's a possible conversation to have with your preschool child about differences.

YOU: Isn't Laura a nice girl?

It's best to start with simple questions like this when you have the opportunity to talk about a specific child who may be different in some way.

HER: Yes, she's nice. Sometimes she's funny.

Children notice differences from a very young age.

YOU: What do you mean she's funny?

It helps to get your child to put her feelings and observations into words so you can talk about them.

HER: She does silly things. She doesn't do things right.

This young girl already has a good sense of doing what's "right," and most preschoolers do.

YOU: Can you tell me about it?

Let her articulate it.

HER: Ms. Katy tells us to point our toes, and has to show her how to do it when we all can do it the first time.

Children at this age will be concrete.

YOU: Does that bother you?

HER: No, but why can't she?

Children want to know about differences because they need to know how they might change from who they are now. They don't know what's fixed and what's not.

YOU: Laura was born with something that makes it harder for her to learn as quickly as you and your other friends.

Keep this simple.

HER: Why?

You have to decide how much detail to give. Best to talk in a general way.

YOU: It happens sometimes that babies are born that way.

HER: Could I be that way?

She needs reassurance that she won't change.

YOU: No, it actually happens before you're born, when you're still in your mommy's tummy.

This will help.

HER: Can you fix her?

It's all part of your child's education.

YOU: Do you think she needs to be fixed?

An excellent question to see how your child thinks about these things and the direction she's going.

HER: Yes. Then she could do things easier. She could dance better.

A very pragmatic answer, not unusual for children this age. They're concerned with doing things right and doing them well, with developing and expanding their abilities.

YOU: Don't you think she dances well?

HER: Yes, but not as good as us.

Children at this age are usually honest.

YOU: Is it okay for her to be different? Do you still like her? Do the other girls like her?

This is a good set of questions for her to think about.

HER: I like her. Other girls like her, too.

YOU: How do you think Laura feels? Does she like you and the other girls? Does she like dancing?

It's always good to get your child to think empathetically; preschoolers can be quite empathetic.

HER: She likes me. She always wants to dance near me, and play, too. She likes dancing.

This is an honest answer you can work with, if you need to.

YOU: I hope you'll always be nice to her and to any other girls and boys who seem different from you.

HER: I will.

A nice ending to the conversation. Let's hope it's like this in real life and continues to be so as your child grows older.

Conversations with School Children

School puts the pressure on kids to fit in. Differences don't cut it for children, especially when they are a little older, like in grade eight. They're not yet teens, but they're no longer innocent first graders. They want to be popular, they need to fit in, and if they don't, if they're different from the other kids for almost any reason, they can be the butt of bullying and teasing.

To combat this, to stand up for themselves, children often form cliques, or become members of clubs and sports teams or student government. This doesn't necessarily help the kids who remain isolated because of physical, personality, or other differences which prevent them from fitting in with a group that would offer them acceptance, comfort, and protection.

A *New York Times* article about a Connecticut middle school described the popularity syndrome amongst eighth graders in this way: "In eighth grade, popularity occupies the same kind of psychic space that sex and money do in the decades to come. And just as the very rich don't like to discuss their wealth, the popular girls in eighth grade get a little uncomfortable when the subject of popularity comes up."

It may make kids uncomfortable to talk about their popularity, but it sometimes makes unpopular kids homicidal, as we saw in the Columbine shootings. This is why it's especially important for you to make sure your children learn to accept differences amongst their peers as natural, normal, and enriching rather than as perverse, abnormal, and a social sin.

You can begin by pressing home the message that everyone who is respectful and considerate of you deserves respect and consideration in return. And even those who are not deserve some attempt at understanding. Your kids need to talk with you about their attitudes and actions toward kids who don't fit in as a way to combat abuse and encourage tolerance. They need to begin thinking about stereotyping, prejudice, discrimination, and scapegoating; how they are different, how they are the same, and what consequences might come from acting toward others in these ways.

The Children Who Are Different or Who Don't Fit In Conversation Script for School Children

"We need to talk"

Here's a way of introducing some important ideas about differences that can make sense to your child and give him some insight into how the neutral label "different" can lead to the pejorative label "different."

YOU: You have brown eyes and brown hair. What would you think if I said that all kids with brown eyes and brown hair were better than kids with brown eyes and blonde hair?

It's always best to start with a fairly innocuous, mundane kind of difference. It's familiar and easy to make sound silly later on.

HIM: That's crazy.

That's usually the initial reaction, but a little probing shows how that can change.

YOU: Why is it crazy?

You need to get these ideas on the table early in your conversation.

HIM: Because the color of your hair doesn't matter, unless it's purple, and then it means you're a Goth or something, and they're no good.

Your unsuspecting boy has begun to get at the real issues.

YOU: Why are they no good?

Now you can begin to build your case by probing his position.

HIM: They're kooky, strange, they wear weird clothes and things. But we don't have any in our school. The high school does.

Kids often don't examine or reflect on their stereotypes or prejudices until they have to.

> YOU: Do you think you can know about people from their hair color?

A good question.

> HIM: Yes, if it's purple.
>
> YOU: What if it's black?
>
> HIM: Only if you dye it black.
>
> YOU: Why black? What about red or blonde? Girls and guys dye their hair different colors.
>
> HIM: It's just that some kids dye their hair to be different and some to be better looking. I don't like the kids who just want to be different.

Kids don't tolerate differences easily. It seems some kind of biological imperative because it's found in all cultures.

> YOU: Why?
>
> HIM: Why do they have to be different?

He takes it for granted that choosing to be different is bad.

> YOU: Isn't everyone different in some way?
>
> HIM: Yes, but not in strange ways.
>
> YOU: What's strange?
>
> HIM: Strange is when you make yourself different when you don't have to be. Kids who are sick, or crippled, or have a mental problem are different, but that's okay because they can't help it. They'd like to be like us if they could, but they can't. Kids who can but don't want to be are strange. We don't like them.

You've got him to open up and state his position in a pretty coherent way. Now you have something you can really work with.

> YOU: Do they like you?

HIM: No, but I don't care because we're the popular group.

YOU: Why should everyone have to be like you?

HIM: Cause we're the best.

YOU: Do you think this is a good thing?

HIM: Yes!

YOU: Have you learned about the lynching of African Americans in the last century and about segregation in the U.S. and apartheid in South Africa? Have you studied the killing of Jews and Gypsies in Nazi Germany in WWII? Have you been told in school about the massacre of hundreds of thousands of one African tribe by Africans of a different tribe in Rwanda? Have you been told about all the times in history when people who thought they were the best started killing all the people they thought were different, people they thought were not even human?

This is where you get serious and start to point out the historical consequences of people believing what he is now saying.

HIM: Some of it.

YOU: Do you think what you're saying is any different? Do you think you're the best and you don't like people who are different from you?

You'd better make this connection if he doesn't see it himself. Children often don't see the larger issues and potential consequences of their prejudices and intolerance toward differences.

HIM: Sure; we're not going to kill people because they're different.

YOU: But that's where it can lead. Would you want that?

HIM: No!

YOU: Then you'd better start thinking about how you and your group feel about kids who have purple hair, or who choose to be different from you simply because they want to be.

You need to spell out the potential consequences.

HIM: Maybe I should.

This is an optimistic ending, but the conversation could just as easily end differently.

In your conversation with your child, make sure you end positively, with a lesson for him to think about.

Conversations with Teens

When my daughter was in high school, she was in a popular clique of girls. They were the prettiest, smartest, and most sought after by the popular boys, who were the athletes.

One of the boys in the school, wasn't an athlete. He was gay, possibly the only gay boy in the school, but certainly the only one who was openly so. He didn't attempt to hide it and as a result, he was teased unmercifully. Until my daughter and her friends decided this had to stop.

They decided they would be his protectors, and they were. The football, basketball, and hockey players were told in no uncertain terms they had to stop this nonsense or they would be ignored by the girls: no dates, no parties—nothing—until they left this boy alone, and it worked, at least on the surface. The other boys stopped teasing him and he and the girls became the best of friends.

There are untold numbers of similar stories about gay high school boys and girls being picked on, tormented, and even driven to suicide by the heterosexual community. Most of the time, little seems to be done by the school authorities to protect these most vulnerable of children.

There are many other stories of teens suffering because they didn't fit into any of the major high school groups or cliques. Some of the lucky ones have found refuge in special-interest groups such as drama or music clubs. One such fellow, who had been an athlete when he was a freshman, quit the football team because he didn't like the way his teammates acted. There was too much pressure to be cool and too much picking on the loners—the kids who were different—who were neither athletes, nor academic stars, not good-looking enough or outgoing enough to be part of the in crowd.

This boy, a musician, joined the drama club and became its president. He loved the people because they were like a family, everyone who loved drama or who participated in it was accepted, regardless of their appearance or talent, as long as they were nice.

While that may sound suspiciously ideal, it does point out there are places where kids who are different can find a home. It also shows kids need a home, a place where they can feel wanted, accepted for who they are, and not laughed at, bullied, or teased.

This only serves to emphasize the need for you to help your teens become accepting and tolerant of differences, if they aren't already so.

The Children Who Are Different or Who Don't Fit In Conversation Script for Teens

"We need to talk"

Homosexuality is an important difference that evokes a host of feelings and conflicting views among various groups. Here's one take on a conversation with your teen about this sexual orientation and his views on this kind of difference.

YOU: Are there many gay kids in your school?

This is as good a way to begin this discussion as any. The mistreatment of gay kids in school is probably one of the major issues needing conversation with your teen because it is a problem in virtually every high school.

HIM: Yes, there are a few, but I don't know any of them very well.

Distancing himself from gay kids helps him ignore their problems.

YOU: How do the other kids treat them?

HIM: Most of us just ignore them, but some kids go at them, especially the ones that are obvious, the "flamers" we call them.

Hopefully, your son isn't one of the bullies. But you need to explore this possibility.

YOU: What do they do?

You want to know how much your son has seen of this.

HIM: Call them names, maybe take their hats, scarves, or books, write things on their lockers, text them "evil" messages, or put out things about them online. Some kids try to get them to fight, but mainly it's calling them names.

It's quite a catalogue of things.

YOU: Does anyone try to stop this? Teachers? The principal? Other kids?

Good question, as you can use it to take you further into the abuse of gay kids and the insensitivity and inaction of some school personnel.

HIM: Only if they fight them. Then the teachers will stop it. The kids never interfere.

This is, unfortunately, too common.

YOU: Do you ever try to stop this kind of treatment of your schoolmates?

You have to decide how much you want to ask your son to get involved, and in what way.

HIM: They're not my friends; they just go to the same school.

YOU: Do you feel nothing for them when other kids have a go at them?

HIM: Not really—it's their choice to have a gay lifestyle.

Now we get to the heart of one of the big issues about differences and not fitting in. It's the belief that people, especially homosexuals, choose not to fit in, to be different, to pursue a deviant lifestyle, and that justifies their persecution, alienation, and rejection.

YOU: Do you really think it's a choice?

You need to know where you stand on this issue, and why. This is a good question because you need to know what your son believes.

HIM: Sure! Don't you?

YOU: No, I don't.

HIM: Well, I do and so do lots of kids. Why can't they just be normal like us?

It's the old "normal" thing. We are normal, others who are not like us are abnormal, and we can reject them because they have rejected the opportunity to be normal like us. So they deserve everything they get.

YOU: Did you choose to be the way you are? I mean heterosexual?

This is where you can really get your son to examine the issue of choice.

HIM: No, I didn't have to because that's the way I am. It's normal.

YOU: Could you have chosen to be gay?

HIM: Hell, no!

YOU: Then why do you think they chose to be gay?

HIM: Because straight is normal.

YOU: You're not understanding me. What I want to know is why you think being gay is any more of a choice than being straight? In other words, if you didn't choose to be straight, why do you think they chose to be gay? I repeat, why is being gay any more of a choice than being straight?

HIM: Well, I don't know. It just is.

As long as your son believes this, he won't be swayed to help prevent the abuse of gay kids.

YOU: Look at it this way: Why would anybody choose to be gay when it exposes them to all the terrible treatment you described? It doesn't make any sense. And it doesn't make any sense to say that being gay is a choice but being straight is not.

HIM: Well, maybe you're right.

YOU: You bet I'm right. There seems to be more and more evidence piling up that sexual preference is not a choice, that certain chemicals in the brain determine it. But even if that were not the case, it doesn't justify the way your classmates are treated by some kids, and I hope you won't just stand by and let this happen. At least try to get other kids to protect these kids, and get the teachers and administrators to do the same thing.

HIM: Maybe I can do something. I know it's not right.

Let's hope your son is this sensible and sensitive.

YOU: I'm glad to hear you say that.

Chapter 6

Proper Behavior Toward the Opposite Sex

DURING THE CHRISTMAS holidays, we had most of our children and grandchildren over to the house. After some hours of contented playing in the playroom, one of our granddaughters came upstairs crying real tears. The boys were roughhousing, and she accidentally got hit. Her crying made her brother angry and he said she couldn't be a member of his family. This was more than she could bear, and the crying became more sadness than physical hurt.

Another story about the loss of innocence amongst younger children was told to me by one of my students. It took place at a Halloween celebration in the seventh-grade elementary school class where he was a student-teacher. He and his partner teacher decided to have a class party and told the children they could come in costume, assuming they would see ghosts and witches, princesses and warriors, video game and TV characters. They got something that shocked and surprised them.

Apparently, the big Hollywood film for the preteen female set that year was *Mean Girls*. At a big party, the "mean girls" dressed up as sexy versions of animals: a sexy cat, a sexy mouse, and a playboy-like bunny. The costumes were very revealing and provocative, making them look more like exotic dancers than students attending a costume party. Can you guess what costumes my student's seventh graders wore?

Yes! They came dressed like the girls in the movie, to the shock and chagrin of their teacher and my student. In part, this is a case of adults underestimating the understanding young girls have of their own sexuality and the power it gives them. Seventh-grade girls are on the edge of or just beyond the beginning of puberty, so one can understand their awareness of physical and emotional changes, but even younger girls seem to understand the important physical differences between boys and girls and the power that gives to them. This awareness speaks to some of the issues surrounding proper behavior toward the opposite sex. There are many others, of course.

As a parent, you have the main responsibility for teaching by example and telling and discussing what is and is not proper behavior. You have to start young because at a very young age children separate themselves by gender and role. Whether by nature or nurture, gender identities and roles become strong influences on the way children include and exclude other children from certain social roles, affiliations, and physical activities.

You may not agree with how your own and other children decide that boys can do this and girls can do that and boys can't do this and girls can't do that, but in the midst of this kind of social development, you can do something very positive. Teach your children that the opposite sex always deserve respect and consideration, just like members of their own gender. You can teach them they must never mistreat other girls or boys for any reason. You can teach them they must never stand around and let other boys mistreat girls, or girls mistreat boys. In other words, watching mistreatment is not an option. They must intervene or report the mistreatment to someone who can. Finally, you need to model this behavior of respect and consideration.

We have all seen, heard, or read about cases of spousal abuse. In many cases, it's the husband abusing the wife, but it does happen the other way around as well. If you accomplish nothing more in teaching your children proper behavior toward the opposite sex than ensuring they will never abuse their partner or spouse, you will have done one of the most important things you could possibly do for them and for society.

Conversations with Preschoolers

When my grandson was in playschool, he had lots of friends and seemed to enjoy playing with girls every bit as much as with boys. I think he might have even enjoyed playing more with the girls in his class. But there were times when he and one of my other grandsons would exclude my granddaughter from games.

Even four- and five-year-old children sometimes do the "boys against girls" thing. It doesn't matter as long as it stays innocent and peaceful, benign and not hurtful, but as soon as it hurts others physically or emotionally, you'll want to step in and smooth things over. Your child should never be allowed to be physically aggressive with or exclude the opposite sex from games, playing with toys, or from running games or sports. At this age, the physical differences between the genders is insignificant, while the intellectual differences can be seen in the verbal fluency of girls compared to boys, superior fine-motor skills in girls, and an overwhelming physicality in boys.

These similarities and differences need a passionate and attentive hand from you to keep them from causing one gender to conspire against or physically abuse the other.

The Proper Behavior Toward the Opposite Sex Conversation Script for Preschoolers

"We need to talk"

If you can lay the foundation for respect and appreciation of boys for girls and girls for boys at this age, you will have gone a long way to ensuring your child understands how to behave toward the opposite sex. Here's an example of what your talk about this tough topic might sound like.

YOU: Don't hit your cousin.

At this age, you must be clear and direct. First the rule, then a discussion about why it's a rule.

HIM: But she's bothering me.

A familiar cry, but one that can mean so many different things. You have to assess its meaning in each new situation.

YOU: I don't care if she is bothering you; hitting is not the way to make her stop.

Good move. Regardless of the situation, certain remedies, like hitting, are always unacceptable.

HIM: Yes it is.

Technically, he may be right, but morally he's wrong and you have to show him why.

YOU: Listen, please. We've talked about this before, do you remember?

He may not remember, but that doesn't matter. It's a good excuse to go through it all again.

HIM: No.

Truth or not, it doesn't matter; that's not the issue. The issue is what has just happened and how to prevent it from happening again.

YOU: Well, let me remind you. We talked about certain rules of playing with girls and with boys, and we said certain things about what do to if you're unhappy. Can you tell me what they were?

This is setting up the context for what comes next.

HIM: No, I don't remember.

YOU: Let me help you. Do you remember what we said about hitting?

Physical violence against children in general, and girls in particular, tops the agenda.

HIM: No hitting.

YOU: Good. Who don't we hit?

It's a good move to get him to say it, not just listen to you saying it.

HIM: We don't hit girls.

YOU: Who else don't we hit?

HIM: We don't hit boys.

YOU: Why don't we hit girls?

HIM: Because it will make them cry.

YOU: Yes. Why else?

HIM: Because it's not nice to hurt people.

YOU: That's right. And why don't we hit boys?

HIM: Because it will make them cry and hurt them.

YOU: So, we don't hit. What else don't we do to girls?

The hitting rule is well established. Now to move on to the psychological and emotional abuse that children use so skillfully.

HIM: We don't call them names.

YOU: And what else?

HIM: We don't tease them or push them or tell them they can't play just because they're girls.

This is a good list of the don'ts, but saying it once or having him say it is never enough. You have to repeat this after every new situation until he's tired of hearing it, or the bad behavior stops.

YOU: What else?

HIM: We don't take toys from them.

YOU: If you want to play with one of the toys they have, what do you do?

HIM: You say, "Please may I play with your toy?" We can share.

YOU: That's good. You remembered a lot. Do you remember why we have these rules?

You want to hear it from his lips. You saying it is not enough to cement it into his memory.

HIM: Because boys should never pick on girls. Boys should be good to girls so girls will be good to them.

It may not be the best reason in the world, but it's good enough for the moment with preschoolers.

YOU: That's close enough. Very good.

This is a good start. Keep working on it.

Conversations with School Children

When my grandson was in first grade, he had a crush on a fifth-grade girl. I had my first crush on a girl, as far as I can remember, when I was in third grade. I even remember having strange dreams about her. Nature has made sure that the dance of life starts very early.

Boys and girls don't have trouble giving special attention to each other, sometimes as special friends, sometimes with a baby crush. Sometimes, this attention gets mixed in with too much hostility and aggression. I don't remember clearly how I thought about girls when I was in school, but I do remember feeling strong emotions toward them that only intensified as I grew older. I wanted to be noticed, to be liked, to be wanted by them, even in elementary school. I can't imagine that I was much different from any other boy in my class, and I presume girls wanted to be noticed, liked, and wanted just like boys.

The Proper Behavior Toward the Opposite Sex Conversation Script for School Children

"We need to talk"

The challenge for parents is to channel these needs appropriately so they manifest themselves in socially and physically considerate behavior toward the opposite sex. Here's an example of what a conversation about this behavior might sound like.

HER: I like James, but I don't know if he likes me.

A typical schoolgirl concern. These days, with text messaging, Facebook, and instant messaging, it may be less of a problem than it was in my school years.

YOU: Why don't you ask him?

Sounds like good advice to me. Don't beat around the bush.

HER: I can't do that.

You need to respect this. She knows her territory better than you.

YOU: Why not?

It doesn't hurt to ask why. Maybe you'll learn something that will help you in the future with this kind of problem.

HER: Because.

This doesn't shed much light on things.

YOU: Because why?

HER: Because I can't.

YOU: Ask his friends.

Sounds like a reasonable suggestion.

HER: I could, but they might laugh at me.

Being laughed at would be a terrible for her. Respect it.

YOU: Why would they do that?

It's good to get her to articulate her feelings. It will help her as much as it will help you.

HER: Because they might think I silly.

Perhaps she's seen this happen to others and doesn't want to be a victim as well.

YOU: No, they wouldn't. You're not a silly girl.

You can reassure her, but it might not help.

HER: Sometimes I am.

A valuable moment of introspection and reflection on past behavior.

YOU: How?

HER: Sometimes I chase him around the playground. Or throw snowballs at him.

If she only knew how normal that is she might not feel silly about it.

YOU: Why do you chase him?

Nice question. You think you know the answer, but you don't.

HER: Just to show him I can run faster than he can.

This is the answer, but not the one you were looking for. She doesn't recognize this for the foreplay it is.

YOU: Can you?

HER: Yes.

If she couldn't catch him you can bet she wouldn't chase him. And maybe he wants to be caught, which makes everything easier.

YOU: Why is that silly?

You know it's not silly and that he would never think it's silly, unless he truly didn't like her.

HER: Because when I catch him I don't know what to do.

She doesn't realize that it's the journey, not the destination, that's important at this stage.

YOU: But you're always nice to him, aren't you?

This is the crux of the matter, being nice to him when she catches him.

HER: I try to be, but I pull his coat and he falls down, or I pull his scarf or take his hat, and he chases me because he wants them back.

This will definitely make him notice her.

YOU: But you never hurt him, do you?

It doesn't hurt to press home this message.

HER: No, I never do.

YOU: You know that you must never do anything to hurt someone, especially a boy you like, or even one you don't like.

Again, and again, and again, you can never say it often enough: no hurting.

HER: I wouldn't, but some girls do. They make them cry.

YOU: That's awful.

No need to hide your feelings.

HER: Yes. I don't like it. I try to help them.

If only all children did this.

YOU: Who, the boy or the girl?

You knew whom she meant, but you're doing this for emphasis.

HER: The boy. Even if I'm chasing him, too. I never want to hurt him.

YOU: You're a good girl. I know you would never purposely hurt a boy.

HER: No, I wouldn't.

Conversations with Teens

This where you have the most responsibility for ensuring your teen respects the opposite sex in every way, because at this age boys can do great physical damage to girls and girls can destroy a boy's confidence and feelings of self-worth.

When I was a junior in high school, I went to a party of friends. I was very shy and had little confidence in my attractiveness to girls. Among the people I met there was an older girl, probably a senior. For some reason, which I couldn't figure out, she came on to me in a very strong way. I remember feeling quite flattered by it all.

She asked me about myself, what I did at school, what my plans were, what I liked and didn't like in movies and music. She wanted to know about me in ways no other girl ever had. I went home that night feeling great about the party and myself.

The next day, one of my friends told me that it had all been a joke. The girl was the older sister of one of the guys at the party and he and some other guys and girls had convinced her to pretend to come on to me. Of course, they were delighted I had been completely taken in by it. Eventually they all apologized, including the girl, and we remained friends, but I remember that incident to this day with shame and embarrassment.

This story represents a rather harmless prank, but it shows the emotional power girls can exercise over boys. Boys, on the other hand, have a physical strength that can inflict untold harm on girls. Both genders must be aware of their powers and use them with care and sensitivity toward each other.

One last story to bring home the point. A friend of one of my sons was in a relationship with a girl when they were in high school. She decided the relationship was too emotionally difficult and tried to break it off. He refused. She told him she didn't want to see him again. One evening, he broke into her home in order to talk to her. She and her mom were out and found him there when they got home. He wouldn't leave, so they called the police, who made him leave.

Then, the girl got a court restraining order against him. It didn't work—he again broke into her house. The police were called again and he was taken away and spent the night in jail. Nothing else came of it—no physical violence—but my son's friend did spend some time in counseling. He was a loving boy, he loved this girl, but he couldn't control his emotions and his anger when his emotions caused her to break up with him. As I said, there was no violence, but with other boys, there could have been.

The Proper Behavior Toward the Opposite Sex Conversation Script for Teens

"We need to talk"

Once again, I'm going to give you a conversation that you can use as a model. This is a conversation with a boy because boys need to learn to exercise the most control in their relationships with girls because of the physical, as well as emotional, damage they're capable of doing.

> **YOU:** This is a conversation we should have had a while ago, before this trouble began.

It's better to have it late than not at all.

> **HIM:** What trouble?

Evasion of responsibility, or feigned ignorance, is not an unusual response.

YOU: You, breaking into her house in order to see her after she told you she didn't want to see you again.

There's no point in beating around the bush. Tell it like you see it.

HIM: Oh, that. It was nothing.

Failing to admit guilt, a mistake, or poor judgment is normal and tells you you have a lot of work to do to make him see the error of his ways.

YOU: The police picked you up and you spent the night in jail. I don't call that nothing.

HIM: They didn't have to do that; I'd have left.

Then, the obvious question is, why didn't you?

YOU: But you didn't, and you violated a court order. You can't go around doing that.

These are the facts and he needs to face up to them.

HIM: She shouldn't have gotten a court order.

Again, a denial of the seriousness of the problem. There's little hope of him addressing a problem if he refuses to admit it even exists.

YOU: What was she supposed to do?

You're trying to look into his mind and see what he's thinking.

HIM: Just told me to stay away.

Under the circumstances, not much of a solution.

YOU: She did that, but it didn't work.

Another fact in this case he ignores.

HIM: I just wanted to talk to her.

This may be true, but it wasn't the issue. The issue was violating a court order.

> YOU: But she didn't want to talk to you.

> HIM: But I needed to explain things to her. She wouldn't listen.

You can see how his emotions are controlling his thoughts and preventing him from seeing the seriousness of the situation and the fact that he broke the law.

> YOU: Look, she's a lovely girl, we all like her and we can understand you liking her, but she decided she couldn't cope with your moods. There were too many other things she had to deal with, she didn't need to deal with your problems, too.

You can try to put the problem into this context and see if he understands what you're saying. If he does, good; if he doesn't, you have to keep working at it.

> HIM: I just wanted her to listen. We could have worked things out.

He still doesn't get it.

> YOU: I think it was too late for that.

> HIM: If only she would have listened.

> YOU: You never did anything to her, did you?

There was no evidence that he did, or would, but you want the issue on the table anyway.

> HIM: No, I would never do that, ever.

There's no evidence or history to suggest that he would be violent.

> YOU: I don't think you would.

You should show that you believe him.

> HIM: I just wanted to be with her.

Yes, and that desire trumped everything.

> **YOU:** Well, you went about it the wrong way. Do you understand why?

You're still working on getting him to see what happened through others' eyes.

> **HIM:** No.

That's obvious.

> **YOU:** When you love someone, and I think you love her, you can't treat them like you own them. You have to give them space, a life separate from the relationship with you. You can't bring all your problems to them and not accept they have problems to cope with, too, and they can't do that when you're hopelessly suffocating them.
>
> In your love for her you forgot to give her the respect she deserved, you forgot about her needs, her self-worth, you forgot about being kind to her, respecting her independence, and your responsibilities toward her.
>
> You only saw things from your point of view, not hers, and now you've paid the price for it. Do you understand?

You are laying it out for him in as clear a way as you can. If he doesn't see it, you will have to keep trying, or let the police and the courts deal with him.

> **HIM:** I guess.

Only time will tell if he really understands.

Chapter 7

Toys, Clothes, and Money

I'M WRITING THIS chapter at the end of the Christmas season, a time when untold amounts of money are spent on giving children toys they don't need, may not even want, or if they do want them, they tire of quickly. These toys were probably destined for the scrap heap even before they were given, and will end up in the trash or being given away.

I don't mean to condemn toys or Christmas gift giving. As a child, I used to wake up as early as 4:00 A.M. on Christmas morning because my anticipation of new and wonderful toys made it impossible for me to sleep any more. I still love the joy and excitement of Christmas morning—watching children unwrapping their gifts, as well as the gift I have chosen for my wife.

Children and toys are an extremely difficult and touchy subject because we all want the best for our children and we want them to be happy. We can see their happiness when they get a new toy they wanted, even if that happiness is fleeting.

Nevertheless, there is an important social aspect to children's toys. For them, having a toy their friends have, or that their friends would like to have, is an important part of their relationship building and relationship sustaining with other boys and girls. Boys and

117

girls spend much of their nonschool hours playing. Play is done through words, deeds, and objects and toys often provide the focal point for the games children play. It doesn't matter what kind of toy it is as long as it's the right one. Children, as a group, decide which toys are the desirable ones. Your child doesn't have that power, nor do you.

Toys represent more than themselves and that's what can make them problems for you in your relationship with your children. They represent pride of ownership, status within the child's group, and a source of pride, pleasure, and affiliations with other children.

To some extent, clothes do the same thing. Your child shows membership, status, and understanding of social norms by being a slave to fashion as much as you are with your own age and social group. Even preschoolers pay attention to what their friends wear or to what they think best suits their personal self-image. Yes, pre-schoolers have very strong self-images.

As children grow up, their concern with clothes will be more specific and dictated largely by what the kids in their identity group at school wear, which, in turn, can come from many different sources, most obviously films, games, and video and computer images.

Your challenge as a parent is to make sure what they want to wear is affordable, acceptable, and appropriate. An increasing number of schools cope with this situation by making uniforms mandatory for kids, or by having strict dress codes.

Dolly Parton is reputed to have quipped: "Whoever said that money can't buy happiness doesn't know where to shop." Whether she said it or not, it's an amusing idea, and it reflects the attitude most of us have toward money. The more money the better, because with money comes purchasing power, and buying things means making us happy by satisfying our wants as well as our needs. We know that happiness comes from owning things, at least until the next, newest, and better things come along.

Money starts motivating children when they become consumers. Ads target children very effectively and help them develop a strong sense of what they want and don't want to buy. Buying, they soon realize, requires money. And money, for young children, usually comes from parents, relatives, Santa Claus, and the tooth fairy, in the form of allowances, payment for chores, gifts, and rewards. That means that you, as a parent, are the first line of information and education about the value and perils of money.

Talking to your kids about money often means being open with them about family circumstances. Of course, it needs to be age appropriate, but it can include, in general terms, income and expenses, sources of income and reasons for expenses, and the choices we all have to make when we try to balance our budget. It's a good way to begin discussing the differences between needs and wants, a distinction children often ignore or misunderstand.

Your biggest and most important job in educating your children about money will be talking and living a set of values that emphasize what is essential to happiness, and what is unessential. We all also know that ultimate happiness must be independent of wealth and material objects, and can only be found in self-discovery, understanding, and relationships—things that money can't buy. That's where your talk should be heading, even with young children, but you also have to model this yourself. If you're greedy and very materialistic, your children will likely be the same.

Conversations with Preschoolers

The conversation with preschoolers needs to be about toys and, maybe, clothes. Money for kids this age is typically not an issue except as it pertains to your ability to buy your children the most recent toy they want.

Clothes are much more of an issue for little girls than for most little boys. This sounds like a stereotype, but I promise you, it's true, for whatever reason. Partly, I suppose, because the range of fashions for girls covers everything from pants to dresses, and from everyday dresses to party dresses, even for three- and four-year-olds. Moms and grandmothers fuel part of this obsession. My take on it is that women love playing with dolls as mothers and grandmothers as much as they did as children, and new girl babies are the closest thing to dolls they can get at their age.

Most boys wear whatever is handy, and buying clothes for them comes more from the need for utility than for fashion. Boys' clothes need to be durable, washable, and masculine, even for four- and five-year-olds.

The real issue surrounding conversations with preschool boys and girls around clothes is cost and lifespan. Kids this age grow so fast that buying new clothes seems a waste of money. Kids grow faster than fashions.

Stereotypical as it may seem, conversations about clothes and toys makes more sense when you talk to girls about clothes and to boys about toys. The following conversation reflects that.

The Toys, Clothes and Money Conversation Script with Preschoolers

"We need to talk"

This conversation script involves a parent and two children, a boy and a girl, as the parent tries to juggle the demands the kids are making for a "must have" toy, and a "must have" dress.

HIM: I need some Legos.

It's a great toy for children, as they can be as creative with it as they want to be, or they can follow the plans, which takes careful attention and understanding, both cognitive skills they need to develop.

YOU: Why? You just got some at Christmas.

HIM: I need the rocket ship and the Terminator.

YOU: Why do you need them?

HIM: All my friends have them.

This is a standard answer for most of kids' needs and wants.

YOU: If they have them, why do you need them? Can't you play with their Legos?

There's always a limit on this kind of sharing, and your child can't take it home with him.

HIM: No. I want my own.

YOU: I'm sorry, but that's not going to happen. You will have to play with the toys you have or with your friends' toys; we're not buying anything new for a while.

This needs to be an honest reflection of your circumstances and your priorities, as well as the kind of attention to financial responsibility you want to develop in your child.

HIM: Why? My friends have them.

A typical response.

YOU: I can't speak for your friends' parents, but we have bought enough toys for the moment and we're not buying any more. But, I have an idea. If you want to spend your own money, you can buy whatever you like. You have money from Christmas and your birthday and from the tooth fairy. You can get more by clearing up your room and helping clean up your playroom.

These are very reasonable ways for your child to earn money.

HER: Can I spend my money to buy what I want, too?

It's an important part of her growing up to understand the value of money.

YOU: I suppose so. What do you want?

There should be no hesitation about this from you. If they earn it, they should be able to spend it as they wish, or to save it.

HER: I want the princess castle and tables and chairs.

YOU: Do you think you have enough money for that?

This is an excellent start to helping her understand the costs of her toys.

HER: I don't know. Can you help me count?

YOU: Yes, I can help you. I can also make the same offer to you as I did to your brother. If you help clean up around the house, I'll pay you some money.

It would be wrong not to give her the same opportunities as her brother.

HER: I will, I will!

YOU: Okay. Just remember that any more toys or clothes have to be bought by you. I'm not spending any more money on this stuff right now—you already have too much, especially when there are children in this country and the world who don't have any.

This is a new and important issue for them to consider.

HER: They can have my old stuff.

HIM: And mine, too. I don't play with some stuff anymore.

YOU: That's very kind of you. I think we'll take some time tomorrow going through all your old toys and clothes. Some of the clothes will go to my friends for their kids, but the toys and some clothes we can take to the women's shelter. You can come with me.

An excellent plan, one which more parents and children should follow.

HER: I want to come.

HIM: Me, too. I'm going to go through my toys now.

HER: Me, too.

YOU: I'm glad you want to do this. Lots of kids your age don't have enough clothes, or any toys, and often not enough to eat. You're very lucky children and I think you are really doing the right thing by wanting to share your things with others.

You should encourage them as much as you can and make sure you and they follow through on this idea.

HER: I want to share.

HIM: Me, too.

YOU: I'm proud of you. I think we should do this every year after Christmas. You and I will go through all your toys and clothes and decide which things to give away to other children who need them.

It can become an annual Christmas tradition, one that will benefit everyone and that reflects the real spirit of giving.

Conversations with School Children

One of my sons and his wife took their two boys, ages five and a half and seven, to Disney World. I was surprised to hear that things had changed at Disney, such that it was not as great this time, at least from a parent's point of view.

The problem, simply put, was too much commercialism and merchandizing. He explained that after coming off each ride you were forced to walk down a passage lined on both sides with things for sale pertaining to the characters and theme of the ride or exhibit. How, he asked, can you keep your kids from wanting every T-shirt, toy, book, video game, CD, and DVD they see that features the fantasy world they've just experienced?

He didn't blame Disney; they are a symptom of the disease, not the disease itself. Children, his included, get taught early on to buy into this passion for things that are supposed to make them happy, and which might actually do so for a while, but then fade as a new desire needs to be satisfied.

You are continually faced with your school children wanting more clothes, toys, allowance, trips, movies, electronics, and games. The call for the simple life, which never existed for us any more than it did for our children and now our children's children, awakens a noble sentiment in us that is more fiction than reality. We're all victims of our success in producing a world intent on satisfying the wants, not needs, of its growing population at the expense of everything else.

How do you talk to your school kids about all of this without sounding like a hypocrite to yourself? If you're anything like me, you're hooked on material comforts and all the luxury and ease that money can buy. But I do want to suggest how you can talk to your school children about toys, clothes, and money, which might make sense to them and temper some of the desperate need they may feel to have more of all three.

The Toys, Clothes, and Money Conversation Script with School Children

"We need to talk"

The goal of this script is to help parents teach their children the difference between need and want.

YOU: I think we need to talk about some things that are really important to you, and to me too, but in a different way. Are you okay with that?

You should have this talk with them at some point, perhaps best when they've asked you for something.

HIM: What is it?

YOU: I want to talk about the things you talk about and want to buy and the money you need to buy them, things like toys and clothes.

School children are of an age you can talk seriously with them about things that cost money, where the money comes from, and why there's not a limitless supply. This can lead you to talk about their priorities and yours.

HIM: Like what?

YOU: I guess I want to talk to you about the toys you have and always want more of, the clothes you say you need because other kids have them, and money, which you think we have in endless supply, which we don't. I need to talk about these things because we need to put some limits on things now that you are getting older and can understand why you can't have everything you want. I put it this way because I think you get everything you need, but everything you want is a very different thing.

You must make the difference between wants and needs explicit in your talk to them about spending money on things.

HIM: Why do we have to talk about them?

This is a fair question from him. He has never thought about it in those terms before. For him, everything is a need.

YOU: Because I think we need to agree there is a difference between what you need and what you want, and I would like to make sure we both understand the differences between these two things in the same way.

It's good to make the issue clear and specific.

HIM: Okay. What's the difference?

YOU: Before I tell you what I think, why don't you tell me what you think?

Let him think about what it might mean.

HIM: Okay. What I need is what I can't do without and what I want is what I can do without but would like to have.

Let's hope your child is as sophisticated as this one, but don't worry if he's not. You can help him along.

YOU: That's great. I think you've gotten it right the first time. Now, can you give some examples? Let's start with clothes.

HIM: Yes. I need underwear, pants, shirts, sweaters, jackets, shoes and socks, and hats for school and stuff to dress up in for parties and other things. I need runners, sweats, uniforms, and equipment for the sports I play, like football, hockey, and basketball. That's about it.

YOU: Good. Now, how much of this stuff do you need?

This is a great issue to discuss because need has as much to do with "what" as it does with "how much."

HIM: Enough so I don't have to wear dirty stuff.

YOU: And where can we buy this stuff?

You're angling toward the designer label versus the bargain store dichotomy.

HIM: The clothes you can get at the department stores and the sports stuff at the sports stores.

YOU: Do you worry about the labels on these things, or the colors, or the design? In other words, how fashionable do they have to be?

This is bound to be an issue sooner or later, as your kids become more fashion conscious as they get older.

HIM: They need to be things the other kids at school won't laugh at. That's a real need; I don't want to look like a nerd.

This is an important concern and you ignore it at your peril. Kids need to belong and they mustn't be exposed to ridicule or teasing.

YOU: Do they have to be new, or can they be hand-me-downs from cousins and my friends' kids?

HIM: I don't care as long as they're nice and in good shape.

YOU: You're a good guy.

You can never go wrong praising your child when praise is deserved. Don't take your child's goodness for granted.

HIM: I know.

YOU: What about toys?

HIM: I need electronic games, a computer, a cell phone, and an iPod.

He's certainly right about the computer, if you don't already have one. The electronic games and iPod are certainly a need for his generation. If he's in junior high school, he may be right about the cell phone, too.

YOU: Why are those needs?

HIM: Because all my friends have them and if I don't have them I end up on the outside and can't talk to my friends.

He will almost always define himself and his needs by comparing himself with his friends. You can't change or avoid that.

YOU: So you think that's a real need, and not just a want?

HIM: It's a need because I want to have friends, and if I don't have them, I won't have my friends anymore.

He's probably right, as shallow and trite as that may seem. But, think of how you define yourself and your needs and wants—you probably compare yourself to your friends as well.

> YOU: Okay, now let's talk a little about money. You get an allowance and you earn money by doing things around the house. I think you and I should sit down and do a budget for you and then you can see how much you have to spend on wants, since we take care of your needs.

You should help him budget his money by listing wants and needs and prices and income. Learning how to keep a record of all his expenditures each week will help him see where his money goes.

> HIM: That sounds great. You buy the needs; I buy the wants.
>
> YOU: That's the deal for now.
>
> HIM: I'm in for that.

Conversations with Teens

In my book on communicating with teens, *How to Say It to Teens*, I have a chapter on talking to teens about money. I start off with a quote from the comedian Jackie Mason: "I have enough money to last me the rest of my life, unless I buy something." I'm sure most teens feel this way about money—they never have enough for needs or wants. Teens have many of both because the pressure is on them to conform to the group they belong to and that includes dressing the way the group does, eating the food the group eats, going to concerts, movies, and parties the group goes to, and having transportation the group approves of. It can also mean playing the sports of one's group, having the electronic toys the group likes, owning and playing an instrument, and going out with the group.

One thing is certain: All of this costs money, usually more money than the average teen has. Teens are at a stage where they want more and more control over their own lives, and money means control.

The Toys, Clothes, and Money Conversation Script with Teens

"We need to talk"

The best topic for this conversation is money, since it covers the other two as far as you and your teens are concerned. Whether you are rich or poor, financial responsibility and accountability must be a major concern for you with your teenage kids. This script involves you and your teen talking about the proper attitude toward money and its sources and uses.

HER: I desperately need some new clothes.

She's probably not kidding; she will feel fashion pressure much more than her brother.

YOU: Why? You got new clothes at the beginning of the school year.

You're just saying this. You know the real issues here are her peer group and the pressures they put on each other to be up to date with the latest fashions for teens.

HER: But things have changed. Fashions have changed.

She'll know more about this than you do.

YOU: Not that much, I hope. I'm sure you can make do with what you have until next year.

You're saying this, but you already know her answer to your objections. You have to figure out a way that she can satisfy her constant need for new clothes and not break your bank.

HER: No, I can't. I'll be laughed at.

Or worse.

YOU: Surely not. Are your friends that shallow?

You've been a teen yourself. You know what they're like.

HER: They're not shallow, but they stay right on top of the latest trends.

YOU: Well, their parents must be made of money to keep up. We're not, so I'm afraid you'll have to keep wearing last week's fashions unless you can save up enough money to buy them yourself.

This is the real issue. You can't, or won't, pay for all these new things.

HER: Can you increase my allowance?

This is a first option, which you can accept or refuse. If you accept, it means she'll have to budget carefully.

YOU: We already give you as much as we can afford. You just have to learn to budget your money better. Of course, you could always get a part-time job. If you got a retail job, you might also get a discount on your clothes.

This is the second option. It's often a good idea, as long as it's safe and schoolwork, sports, and extra-curricular activities don't suffer. Sometimes it's a great incentive to improve schoolwork because retail sales jobs are often very dull and your teen will realize that without a college education, she may end up selling clothes for a living.

HER: But what about my schoolwork?

YOU: Maybe if you had less leisure time you'd do better because you would have to budget your time better. I know that I'm most efficient and productive when I have too much to do.

This is often a side benefit as well.

HER: I might need a ride to and from work if I do get a job.

YOU: Don't worry about that. We'd make sure you got there and back. It would probably only be on the weekends and maybe a day or two after school.

Your help will definitely be needed and appreciated, at least at the beginning.

HER: Okay, I'll try it.

YOU: Excellent. We'll make sure your schoolwork doesn't suffer. If it does, you'll have to give up the job and make some extra money some other way. Maybe by helping us more around the house.

HER: I'll start calling around this afternoon.

Chapter 8

Schoolwork

IN CONVERSATION THE other day with my brother-in-law, he told me about going to dinner parties where the main topic of conversation with the other guests was how to make sure their two- and three-year-olds would be able to get into the right nursery school, preschool, kindergarten, and elementary school. This involved expensive use of consultants, I.Q. testing, and tutors and coaches who would shepherd the child and parents along the hazardous route to opening the door to the "best" and horrendously pricey school for their kids.

The *New York Times* carries regular stories in the spring and fall issues of the competition amongst high school students for admission to the colleges of their choice. The pressure is on for them to do all the normal things we used to do, such as getting high grades and participating in sports and other extra-curricula activities like clubs and student government. But now, the emphasis is on advanced placement courses, in the International Baccalaureate program, or similarly high-level academic programs in the school which include advanced studies in math, science, philosophy, history, and foreign languages that meet an international standard of excellence in content and practice.

Parents seeking a good education for their children look to the public and private systems and home schooling as possible alternatives in an effort to find the best they can afford in what they perceive as an increasingly competitive world for their children. All of this has to be seen in the context of what parents and governments can afford. For example, the "No Child Left Behind" program of the Federal Government was foisted upon the states with inadequate funding, so despite the good intentions, public school systems were unable to provide more and better resources to their schools, particularly those in economically poor areas.

In New York City, where there has been a flight from public education by many middle-class parents, the Head of the Board of Education has devised a system of grading schools according to their achievement on standardized tests at particular grade levels. The pressure is on low-performing schools to improve, and this pressure flows from the Board to the district administrators to the school administrators to the teachers. What's left out of this flow chart is the most important element in school achievement—the parents.

You are the people who count most when it comes to your children's success in school because you provide the most essential resources for learning. These are, quite simply, love and attention, security, good food, good medical care, and a respect for schools, teachers, and learning.

Love and Attention

I hear stories that sometimes make me want to cry from students getting their first experience of what it's like to be a schoolteacher facing a room full of children from a range of backgrounds and home life. Tales abound of children whose parents move them from school to school as they move from one rental accommodation to the next; parents who haven't enough money to pay the rent and buy food; children who come to school in winter in flimsy jackets and who haven't had a proper breakfast. I hear about schools in affluent areas where parents never hesitate to tell teachers how and what to teach. I hear about high school children whose life out of school is prostitution, drug dealing, and hustling to make some money in any way they can. These children are often the first to arrive when the school doors open in the morning and the last to leave when the doors close at night, because school is the only place they know will be safe for them.

If you aren't there to give your children love and attention, whom can they turn to? Children seek and need parents to be there for them, to approve and disapprove, to allow and disallow, to hold and hug and kiss them, to admire and praise their accomplishments, to help them when they need help, and to let them try, let them risk, let them succeed, and let them fail. All this happens in a context of love and attention and security.

Security

I heard a program on the radio in which a social worker spoke about children who had run away from home because they suffered abuse at home. The person had spent countless hours counseling these children. The message he got from them was clear: They didn't want new or different parents; they just wanted their own parents to change. Although this was not the case 100 percent of the time, it was the prevailing sentiment amongst these mainly teens. Their parents were their parents, for always.

They yearned for a safe home, free from abuse for themselves and their siblings, free from violence and uncertainty. They, like us all, wanted stability and peaceful relationships in the home. How could they thrive in school, or any place else, when they constantly feared hitting, beating, threats, sexual abuse, and uncertainty about what would happen next?

You, as a parent, need to be the foundation, the rock, the safe haven for your children. You provide the shelter from the storm where supplies of courage, ambition, confidence, and self-esteem can be replenished through the stability you provide for your children. Security is not the physical space in your home; it is your children's knowledge that you cherish them and will keep them safe from hurt and harm.

Good Food and Medical Care

Success in school, as in life, depends on good health. As I said above, my students bring me tales of children coming to school without breakfast. In these schools, breakfast and lunch are provided, because the parents, for whatever reason, have not done it. Schools all over North America are taking steps to ensure students can find nutritious choices in school cafeterias and vending machines. They are abandoning the pop, French fries laden with trans fats, sugar snacks and candy, potato chips, and other calorie-filled vitamin-empty foods.

Schools are requiring children be immunized against certain diseases and health education classes are teaching good eating practices, good health practices, and generally trying to promote a healthy lifestyle.

Many junior and senior high schools teach sex education, including safe sex, birth control, and abstinence. They also include ethical and moral issues in order to put this aspect of health care in its social context. It is sometimes difficult for them to do this, as parents can have quite differing perspectives on many of these issues.

It is up to you, as a parent, to feed your children well and ensure they have basic medical care. Their success in school depends on this.

Respect for Schools, Teachers, and Learning

In the popular imagination, some cultural groups seem to place a higher value on schooling than other groups. Whether or not this is true doesn't matter, because the variations within groups is consistently greater than the variations between groups. Whatever your own cultural identity, it's up to you to demonstrate in word and deed your respect and enthusiasm for schools, teachers, and learning. This doesn't mean a blind acceptance of all the practices you might find in any particular school. In every aspect of our lives, we find some institutions, people, and knowledge better or more important than others. So it is with schools, teachers, and learning. Some schools, teachers, and learning can be better than others, on both an absolute and relative scale.

Your work for yourself and your children is to make sure you know as much as you can about your child's school, curriculum, teachers, and teaching methods. You want a school that puts more emphasis on developing a child's love of learning, which all young children have. You want a school that allows them to pursue this love of learning, while guiding it in useful and important directions.

Conversations with Preschoolers

Writing about having this conversation about school with preschool children, I am reminded of the time I was in elementary school and there was a line on the report card that said "Works and plays well with others." I'm reminded of this category of assessment because, in my opinion, this is what preschool is all about—the socialization of young children. Success in the early years of school hinges on a few basic social skills you want your children to have. Working and playing well with other children is top of the list.

Preschool teachers may be impressed by your child's ability to read, write, or recognize numbers, letters, and words. But if your child acts out his feelings instead of talking about them, constantly fidgets, is aggressive with other children, calls out instead of seeking the teacher's attention by raising his hand, cries too much, doesn't listen to the teacher's instructions or follow the rules, your child will be labeled a problem, too immature, or not ready for real school.

This is the problem many parents face with their boys—much more so than with their girls. We know boys develop verbal skills at a later age than girls, that they find sitting still more of a problem, and that they are generally much more aggressive toward other children than girls are. All of these general characteristics make preschool more difficult for them and for you. This is all the more reason you need to help your boys become more adept by talking to them on a regular basis. You also need to monitor their behavior with other children, and you need to be firm and consistent in teaching them how to behave toward adults and other children.

You want to compare your child's social skills with those of others and not start your boy in regular school before he's socially ready. For your young boy, schoolwork means learning how to behave appropriately in a group of other children.

The Schoolwork Conversation Script with Preschoolers

"We need to talk"

Here's the kind of talk you can have with your preschooler to help him on his way to success in school. I have purposely made this conversation a talk between parent and son in which your boy is already attending some kind of preschool program.

YOU: I love coming and watching you in your preschool.

Your child will enjoy knowing you take a continuing interest in his schooling, even at this level.

HIM: I like it there.

It's important to know what your child thinks and feels about this experience. Most children like it, but some don't; for those who don't, you need to find out why.

YOU: Your teacher was telling me that sometimes you take things from other children.

We find this kind of behavior in boys far more than in girls, especially in boys whose language development is a bit slower than other boys. They can't act upon their world verbally, so they do it physically.

HIM: No, I don't.

He may not realize what he does is wrong, or that he's doing anything antisocial.

YOU: But your teacher says you do. Can you tell me why you do that?

You might want to refer to specific, concrete instances. Ask his teacher for some.

HIM: It's just because I need it.

This is not necessarily a non sequitur for him; it's just matter of fact.

YOU: What do you need?

HIM: I need a crayon.

YOU: Why can't you ask nicely and see if the other child will share?

If his language development is slow, he may not be able to do this effectively.

HIM: I do, but they say no.

It would be interesting to have been a fly on the wall to see how this really took place.

YOU: Then you should ask the teacher for help. You should never just take something from someone else.

Good advice if he has the ability to follow it. You might want to ask the teacher her opinion of his language-using ability and see if it squares with yours. You might also want to ask her to compare it to other boys his age in the preschool.

HIM: The teacher doesn't listen.

This might be true in some ways. Teachers often ignore children when they are being asked to listen to more than one at a time. Children this age don't know how to wait their turn and may simply give up.

YOU: I'm sure if you are patient the teacher will listen and help you.

In boys this age, patience is in short supply.

HIM: But I try.

He probably does, in his own way.

YOU: Then you need to try harder, and be patient. It's not good to take things from others, and if the teacher is busy, you just have to wait until she can give you her full attention.

It's worth repeating this over and over again.

HIM: But she won't listen.

The same issue repeated.

YOU: You have to wait until she will. Do you know why?

The teacher needs to know how to handle children's competition for her attention so everyone will feel included.

HIM: No.

That's probably quite true.

YOU: Because sometimes people have to wait until others have finished what they're doing and then they can help you. You have to learn to wait for others to be ready. Can you do that?

This is one of the reasons he's in preschool—to learn this skill, which he must have when he starts regular school.

HIM: Yes.

YOU: You need to practice that in preschool and at home, too. When I'm busy, you have to be patient and wait until I'm finished and can help you. Can you try to practice that?

HIM: Yes.

YOU: Please say that in full sentences.

It's better to get him to say it out loud so he gets to practice his English, and he shows in his own words what he understands.

HIM: I can wait until you're finished. Then you can help me.

YOU: That's excellent. What about your teacher? Can you say that about your teacher?

HIM: I can wait until my teacher is finished. Then she can help me.

YOU: Good. Now tell me about taking things from other children. Tell me about asking to share and not grabbing.

Once again, have him say it in his own words.

HIM: I should ask to share and not grab from other children.

This is correct. If your child doesn't say it correctly, stick with it until he does.

YOU: Excellent. What should you do if other children won't share?

A crucial step in the process.

HIM: I should ask the teacher to help me.

Good answer.

YOU: That's right. I think we should write these things down so you don't forget. I will ask your teacher to help you remember these things. We can talk about them every day before you go to school.

Your child may not be able to read these things, but simply putting them down might help bring home the message, and you can go over them every day so he can memorize them, even if he can't actually read them.

Conversations with School Children

School children face some issues that revolve around mastering classroom work and some issues that speak to the male/female differences that may affect how they succeed both academically and socially in school.

Educators, when discussing how schools work, often talk about the "hidden curriculum." They are referring to the routine demands of schooling, which successful children easily master and unsuccessful children fail to learn or seem to ignore or disregard. These include behaving appropriately in and outside class, following the teacher's instructions, obeying school rules, handing in work on time, and showing they are a team player, affirming the values of doing well in school as a prelude to success in life.

Girls seem to be, on the whole, much better at this than boys. While girls and boys in general don't differ much in academic achievement, girls seem able to accommodate to school routine and practices in ways boys often don't. Girls are better "citizens" of the school, but girls differ in classroom participation in ways that are quite noticeable. They simply don't talk as much in class, don't ask or answer as many questions, and generally seem much less self-assertive than the boys in a class.

In talking to your school kids about schoolwork, you can focus on trying to get your girls to take a more active role in classroom discussions to make their knowledge, ideas, and opinions more apparent to the teacher.

The Schoolwork Conversation Script with School Children

"We need to talk"

Here's the kind of conversation you can have with your daughter to accomplish this.

YOU: I was glad to be able to observe your class this year when I volunteered. I think I learned a lot.

142

At this age, your children certainly appreciate your interest in their schooling.

HER: What kinds of things did you learn?

A child in grade two and above can formulate this kind of question.

YOU: I learned that girls should talk more in class.

It's quite an interesting phenomenon—girls not talking as much as boys in class, even though girls' verbal skills are better.

HER: But we're not allowed to just talk in class. We'll get yelled at.

She has misunderstood your point.

YOU: I don't mean that kind of talking. I mean participating in class discussions and asking and answering questions about the things you're learning.

This gives you a chance to clearly state what you've seen and been wondering about.

HER: But I talk a lot. I answer questions and ask them, too. The teacher has told me she's proud of me, the way I talk in class.

This might be, but it must be seen in context. Her talk in class may be good relative to other girls and some boys, but still not as frequent as boys in general.

YOU: That may be, but the days I was there you seemed pretty quiet. Maybe it was because I was there and embarrassing you. I wish I could be there and not be there so I could tell what you're really like in class. But if you're like the other girls, then you're much more quiet than the boys are. It seemed to me like the boys were always volunteering to answer questions while the girls were doing it much less.

She has probably realized this is the case.

> HER: Well, girls don't want to be a smarty-pants.

Yes, it does start this young. Girls don't want to seem to be smarter than boys for fear the boys won't like them. In high school, it gets really bad.

> YOU: What do you mean?

You know very well what she means, but you think it's a good idea for her to spell it out.

> HER: We don't want to show off. Even if we know the answer, we don't want to show we do.

She leaves out the all-important phrase, "in front of the boys."

> YOU: Why not?

Probing is a good idea.

> HER: We just don't.

She won't admit the obvious, although she may not fully realize it.

> YOU: Then why do the boys not care about that?

A fair question, to which you already know the answer.

> HER: Boys like to show off, girls don't.

That's true. Girls compete in a different way.

> YOU: Is answering the teacher's questions showing off?
>
> HER: Sometimes.
>
> YOU: Well, I think you need to show off sometimes because the teacher needs to know that you and the other girls know the answers as much or more than the boys do.

You have stated your case knowing it probably won't get you very far. But it's a beginning.

HER: Why?

YOU: Because the teacher gets a better idea of what you know when you answer questions. If you don't answer, she doesn't know as much about what you're learning.

HER: I guess that's right.

YOU: Will you try to talk more in class, even if I'm there?

HER: I'll try.

YOU: And will you tell your friends that your mom says they should talk more, too, that it's not showing off to answer questions in class?

HER: All right.

There are a number of solutions to this problem. An obvious one is having same-sex classes or schools. Another is self-assertiveness workshops for girls.

Conversations with Teens

Teenagers face a difficult time in high school. Their adolescent brains are pulling them in many directions at the same time. They feel the strains of sexual awakening, infatuation and love, yearnings for independence from parents, the fear of failure in school or not doing well enough to get into the college of their choice, the pressure to conform to the demands of their peers, and the need to assert and express their own personalities and personal style. They deplore the hypocrisy of the older generation and vow to change the world into a better place when have control. They are wise and naïve, mature and childish, strong and weak, independent and dependent, surrounded by peers yet alone.

The Schoolwork Conversation Script with Teens

"We need to talk"

In light of this existential stew, what topic of conversation about schoolwork will serve the best purpose? My experience tells me the most useful talk would be the one that helps your teen leave open as many options as he can at the end of high school. Doing well academically, socially, athletically, communally, and personally does that job. To that end, you might want to have the following conversation with your teenager.

> **YOU:** Are you satisfied with the work you're doing in school this year?

This is a good way to begin, since self-appraisal is a more useful approach than an outsider's appraisal.

> **HIM:** Yes, I'm doing okay.

This is a fairly noncommittal response; it tells you very little. You need to probe further.

> **YOU:** Just okay?

This will do it.

> **HIM:** I like some of my classes and teachers, but not all of them. I think you know that because we've talked about it before.

This is often a problem for teens in school. There is often a great variation in teaching styles and skills, and the subject matter can be boring, or boringly presented. There's much that could be done to get teens involved in their own learning. Some teachers do that very well, but others just follow the set curriculum in a standard, boring way.

YOU: Yes, I know a bit about it, but I think I need to talk about just that issue. I know it's hard to do well in classes you don't particularly enjoy, or with teachers who rub you the wrong way, but I think you know this will happen throughout your life. You'll always have to work with some people you don't like or do some jobs you don't like, but you'll have to do your best nevertheless. That's what I want to talk about with you—always doing your best, and why you need to remember that.

This states the problem in an empathetic and sympathetic way and sets the stage for further discussion of the ways to work around the obstacles your child faces in school.

HIM: What do you want from me?

YOU: I want only what's best for you, because that will make me happier than anything I can think of.

HIM: How do you know what's best for me?

A fairly typical teenage response. It's more a comment than a question. If it's a question at all, it's a rhetorical one.

YOU: Experience. I know a bit more about how the world works than you do, at least in certain areas, and I know that working hard even in lousy situations can pay off in the end.

You choose to hear it as a real question and reply.

HIM: What do you mean, "pay off?" Is everything a matter of money?

Teens pretend to reject materialism until they need new clothes or a car or something else to allow them to keep up with their friends.

YOU: No, not at all; that's not what I meant. I meant that even what seem to be bad situations can have a positive side to them. Trying to do your best in high school and succeeding to the best of your ability can mean you'll be in a position to choose your future in a way you won't if you don't do well. Doing well means giving your best effort in every class, with every teacher, in every subject in your program.

This is a fair statement of the problem and one possible way of approaching it.

HIM: It's not easy. I don't know if I can.

YOU: I know it's not easy—I never said it would be—but it's something you should really try to do. What I'm really talking about are options, your options, when you finish high school. I'm talking about having choices so if you know what you really want you can go after it. For example, if you want to be an engineer but can't get into an engineering program in college because you didn't like your high school math teacher, your high school dislikes have determined your future choices because they've cut down on the options you have.

This is good. You're being realistic and sympathetic while, at the same time, being very pragmatic about actions and their consequences.

HIM: Yes, I see that, but what can I do about it?

YOU: You can adopt an attitude that says you are doing your high school course for yourself, not for your teacher's benefit, my benefit, or simply in order to pass an exam. You're looking at the big picture, not the small one. You're working hard now in areas you may not really like for the sake of what you'll be able to do later when you have the freedom to make life choices.

This is a good motivational approach. Now you have to get your son to buy into it.

HIM: That sounds right, but I don't know if I can do it.

YOU: I'll help you any way I can, but it's really up to you. Only you can do the work and overlook the stuff you don't like. You have to focus on the good stuff and ignore the bad.

You're just reinforcing what you've already said. Now you have to see how your child makes sense of it and whether or not it works.

HIM: It makes sense, but you'll have to keep reminding me, especially when I get caught up in the crap I have to deal with from some of my teachers.

This is as positive a response as you could hope for. Now it's up to him to do it, with your help.

YOU: You come to me and we'll deal with it.

HIM: Okay.

Chapter 9

Choices and Moral Development

BEFORE WE TALK about choices your children have to make, and how to ensure they grow up with a good sense of right and wrong, let's do a short values-clarification question-and-answer session. Here are some questions about general value issues. What are your answers to them?

~ What is your view on birth control?

~ What is your view on abortion?

~ Would you buy and wear clothing made of fur?

~ Are you okay with cloning animals? How about humans?

~ Is it all right to have sex outside of marriage if neither person is married?

~ What about having a baby outside of marriage?

~ Should we allow medical research on stem cells obtained from human embryos?

~ Is medical testing of drugs and other procedures on animals acceptable?

~ Should prostitution be legal?

~ Is pornography okay, even if you don't like it?

~ Should people have the right to kill themselves?

~ What do you think of doctor-assisted suicide?

~ Should we legalize marijuana and other illegal drug use?

~ Is polygamy acceptable? Is polyandry acceptable?

~ Do you accept the principle of gay marriage?

~ What is your view of divorce?

~ What is your view of the death penalty?

According to a recent newspaper article, responses to these questions can put you into one of five different categories, ranging from strict moralist to moral relativist. The categories in between include thoughtful conservative, laissez-faire, and middle of the road. You can easily put yourself into one of these categories according to your views on these questions. Are you a hardliner, a fairly hardliner, a people-should-be-able-to-do-as-they-please-as-long-as-they're-not-hurting-anyone-else kind of person, a none-of-my business-what-others-do kind of person, or a total moral relativist who thinks each situation is unique and must be decided upon in that context?

I suppose it's fair to guess that whatever category you find yourself in, you want to raise your children to have the same views, as these represent your core moral values. However, a number of questions come to mind here. The first, and most important, is what is the source of your values? Are they preached by your religion? Do they come from your experience of the world? Are they simply your strongly held beliefs and understanding of yourself, others, and the world in general? Do they come from your view of humanity and beliefs in right and wrong behavior, without the need of religious doctrine and dogma?

If you give these questions some thought, as your kids grow older, your conversations with them about right and wrong will be substantive and informed because you will have thought through your own beliefs and moral code and will be able to explain where your views come from and why they make sense to you.

Knowing Where Your Child Is on the Moral Development Ladder

Many theories about children's moral development exist. French psychologist Jean Piaget and American moral philosopher Lawrence Kohlberg are two of the best-known theorists on the stages a child goes through in developing her understanding of right and wrong behavior. We are talking about her behavior, rather than what goes on in her head. It's a very pragmatic approach, echoed in the Catholic Church doctrine, "hate the sin, but love the sinner." We can have little direct knowledge of what goes on in anyone else's head, so what we're working with is their behavior, from which we assume certain mental states and beliefs. But that's guesswork and can't be trusted, so it's better to work with behavior.

That's why, when talking about choices and moral development with children, and with young children in particular, you should always tie it directly to some behavior you've observed in him, or in others. You want your son to develop a good sense of right and wrong behavior, right and wrong choices. You can, and certainly will, tie behavior to belief because he will undoubtedly ask you to tie your rules to reasons: Why should I do this? Why should I not do that?

However, your first job should be to make sure your child is behaving properly; then you can work on the reasoning behind it. She might end up hurting herself or others if you spend your time arguing about the reasons for a behavior, rather than stopping the behavior first, then discussing its philosophical source.

In general, we can talk about children's moral development as following a certain path, but this path is not necessarily straight and narrow. It can have little side paths, it can be uphill and downhill, it can circle around and come back on itself, and you can walk on it in at least two directions, backward and forward.

Kohlberg's six stages of moral reasoning are the easiest to follow and seem to have a certain commonsense logic to them. I'll describe the stages using his terms.

LEVEL ONE: Moral reasoning based on personal needs and other's rules

~ Stage 1: He starts with behavior based on a child's needs and other's rules. Children want to please and avoid punishment. They understand good or bad actions by their consequences.

~ Stage 2: Personal needs create what is right and wrong. Moral actions are situational.

LEVEL TWO: Moral reasoning comes from things like the approval of others, family expectations, cultural and religious values, social norms, laws, and patriotism.

~ Stage 3: Good Boy/Nice Girl sums it up nicely. Children look for approval from others.

~ Stage 4: Law and Order Orientation finds morality in authority and societal rules and laws.

LEVEL THREE: Moral reasoning beyond level two.

~ Stage 5: Brings in the notion of the social contract. The good comes from a notion of society's standards that give value to individual rights.

~ Stage 6: Use of universal ethical principles that hold good and right to be matters of conscience and include the concepts of justice, human dignity, and equality.

We can use these general levels and stages to examine how to talk about choices and moral development with our preschoolers, school children, and teens. Level One seems appropriate to kids before and around the age of six; Level Two for preteens and early teens; and Level Three for older teens and adults, hopefully. Each level and its stages give us a clue on tactfully approaching these conversations, using an appropriate tone for each age group.

With Level One, we can focus on obeying rules of behavior inside and outside the family, what makes a child pleasing to adults and other children, and the rewards for such behavior. We must emphasize the actual behavior rather than any abstract reasoning for it, although reasons, of course, should be given.

Level Two focuses on understanding and following some rules and not others, deciding which behaviors are appropriate and why, and how to make use of the laws and customs of society in order to be a good citizen. We need to talk about being a member of our society, making an important contribution

At Level Three we need to encourage them to make sense of their choices and morality for themselves. We need to talk about how we all have to live with the consequences of actions, pointing out that certain conditions may explain bad behavior, but not excuse it. With these children, we can engage in more abstract discussions of ethical and moral principles and values. Help them tell us how they think and make decisions.

Now let's concentrate on how to approach these conversations specifically with each group of children.

Conversations with Preschoolers

You will benefit by being simple, but not simplistic, with your preschool children when you talk about good and bad behavior. Most of this talk will be about doing what mommy and daddy say, not fighting with a sibling or friend, not grabbing toys away from other children, learning the value and practice of sharing, and going to bed at the appropriate time.

In this kind of talk, you need to be concrete and direct. Be clear and consistent, but don't shy away from explaining the reasons why you're telling your child how to think and behave toward others. Above all, in your conversations with your very young children, you want to be consistent and fair, and more importantly, be perceived as being fair. Sometimes, this means explaining your actions or decisions in detail, giving good reasons your child can understand.

You should also make certain your child begins to understand the connection between actions and consequences. The actions of preschool children can be understood as a function of their age, but they should not necessarily be excused from the consequences of those actions. As I said earlier, children of preschool age behave to avoid punishment. As a consequence, you can best teach them moral and ethical behavior by emphasizing the consequences they have to face as a result their actions.

The Choices and Moral Development Conversation Script for Preschoolers

"We need to talk"

Here's a conversation with a preschool child that illustrates the way we teach them good and bad behavior by directly linking their actions toward other children and what they must accept as the consequences of that behavior. Remember that preschool children can show a wide variation in their ability to use and understand language, so you must keep the language ability of your child in mind.

YOU: Please give that back to your little brother.

You can't ignore misbehavior and simply hope it will go away. You need to act.

HER: But I want to play with it now.

Expect resistance. Children this age are very self-centered. That probably has evolutionary value.

YOU: You were playing with it before and now it's his turn.

Don't take any understanding for granted. Ethical/moral behavior needs to be taught through example and in the context of specific instances.

HER: Why? I want it and he's played with it all day.

Be sensitive to your child's sense of time and what's right.

> **YOU:** I don't think so. Please give it back to him.
>
> **HER:** Why can't we share?

This would be a surprising response unless you've taught sharing consistently.

> **YOU:** That's a very good suggestion. I'm glad you think about sharing toys with your brother, but sharing means taking turns and it's his turn.

You should verbally reward this suggestion and take the opportunity to expand on it and clarify it for your child.

> **HER:** No, it's not. It's my turn.

As a parent, you have to sensitively impose your view of reality while trying to create a shared reality.

> **YOU:** No, it's his turn. You've been playing with it since breakfast and it's almost nine o'clock, so it's his turn.

You must have the last word on this and try to show your child why your version is the right one.

> **HER:** But I want to play with it.

You can expect resistance.

> **YOU:** Is it fair if you played with it for thirty minutes and your brother only played with it for ten minutes?

A good question for your child to cope with.

> **HER:** Yes.

Her answer gives you some sense of the state of her understanding. You can work with that.

YOU: How can you say yes? Are ten minutes and thirty minutes the same?

Don't be impatient or amazed; your child is presenting her version of reality.

HER: But he's littler than me.

She's giving back to you a distinction you've probably used in the past to settle problems between your children.

YOU: Does that make any difference in sharing?

This is a test question, meaning that you already know the right answer and you want to see if your child does.

HER: Yes. He's smaller, so he doesn't need to play with it so long.

This makes sense to her. It's her version of a moral law.

YOU: That's an interesting argument, but it doesn't work. Size doesn't make a difference in this case. He can play with it for as long as you did. Then we can start making the time shorter so you can play for fifteen minutes and he can play for fifteen minutes.

You're establishing a new set of rules for your child to work with.

HER: That's not fair.

Your version is rejected, but don't give up.

YOU: It is. It's fair because you both have an equal right to play with the toy. Now, please give it back to him or you'll have to take a time-out in your room.

You've restated the rule and the consequences for your child of not following it.

HER: I don't want a time-out.

YOU: I know you don't, but if you won't do the right thing and share, then you have to face the consequences.

Stick to your guns.

HER: Alright, here it is!

Your child has given in quite unwillingly. Your work has only just begun on her ethical and moral development.

Conversations with School Children

As your children go through elementary school, they will move through stages of moral development. These stages encompass: acting to avoid punishment; acting in one's self-interest; doing something for someone with the expectation of that someone returning the favor; doing things that please, help, or are approved by others; getting appreciation for one's behavior in the form of verbal praise; and doing things out of respect, and perhaps fear, of authority.

All these stages can overlap and come into play in different situations at various times of one's life. They are not discrete, nor are they linear. They coexist in all of us. Adults might have an additional form of moral reasoning that is more abstract, that sees moral behavior as a matter of socially agreed-upon standards of rights and responsibilities and appeals to universal ethical principles of justice, human dignity, and equality. That is not to say school children don't have these moral standards and thoughts as well, they just may not be as fully aware of them.

There are negotiable things in relationships with your children and non-negotiable things. You need to work with your child on what's negotiable and what's not; the distinction might very well be a moral or ethical one. Here's a script that might help you.

The Choices and Moral Development Conversation Script for School Children

YOU: You have to go to school each day whether you like it or not. You do understand that, don't you?

Here's a good situation for you to work with. Your child has a non-negotiable obligation to attend school.

HER: Yes, but I don't have to like it.

She knows you can't make her like it. This, too, is non-negotiable.

YOU: No, you don't, but I wish you did.

You're just stating your true feelings about the situation. You're not trying to change something over which you have little control.

HER: I wish I did, too, but I hate my teacher.

Sadly, this is not an uncommon situation.

YOU: Why do you hate her?

It's worth talking about this to see if there are any clear ways to solve this problem.

HER: Because she's mean to me and the other children.

It's important for teachers to be nice and fair to children and to be perceived as nice and fair. Being perceived as mean, for any reason, will create serious problems in the classroom.

YOU: What do you mean when you say she's mean?

You need to get more information to work on the ethical problem the teacher or the kids may have in this situation.

> HER: She yells at us when we make noise, even though we're still doing our work.

There can be many good reasons, as well as bad, for a noisy classroom.

> YOU: Is that all?

> HER: No. She never teaches us anything, just puts things on the overhead projector and has us copy them down in our books. That's just silly.

This is a real problem in a classroom, as it suggests the social/teaching relationships between teacher and students are not good.

> YOU: Don't you think she's doing the best she can?

Her best may not be good enough.

> HER: If she is, then she shouldn't be a teacher because it's not very good.

She has hit the nail on the head. Good social relationships in the classroom between kids and teacher are the foundation for everything else that's done there, if it's to be done well.

> YOU: But you still have to go to her class every day and do your best.

> HER: I know, but I don't have to like it.

This takes us back to the original problem of the relationship between obligation and true feelings.

> YOU: No, you don't have to like it. There are lots of things you have to do in life that you won't like.

This begins to speak of a certain maturity that your child may not yet have, doing things we dislike now for future rewards.

HER: Why do we have to?

You will need to spell it out for your child.

YOU: Because in the long run, it's good for you to do these things.

Your child may have heard this many times before, but it doesn't hurt to say it again and to fill in the details.

HER: Like what?

YOU: Like brushing your teeth in the morning and at night. Like picking up after yourself and keeping your room reasonably clean and orderly. Like helping with the dishes, garbage, and recycling. Like bathing regularly and keeping yourself clean. Like being nice to people, even those you don't like. Like sharing your toys. And like listening to what your parents tell you.

These are the things that we do that pay off in the end.

HER: Why are those things good to do?

A good question that requires a good answer.

YOU: Because your happiness and the happiness of others depends on our getting along with each other, not fighting, not doing or saying mean things. Because it's better to be healthy than sick. Because it's better to have a clean, safe world than a dirty, dangerous one. Because it's better to share the things you have with others. And because much of what you learn you will learn from experience and your parents already have that experience.

These are things that need much more talk than we can give it here. But you can discuss these moral and ethical imperatives over and over again in each new situation.

HER: But I still don't like having such a bad teacher at school. And I wish that could change.

These nice words haven't caused the original problem to change or disappear. It stills needs serious addressing.

YOU: It's too bad, but you have to make the best of it. Life is not perfect. We make the world better when we work with others to make it so. Maybe you could work with your teacher, instead of against her, to make it better.

You're introducing a collaborative approach to the problem, which is better than simply trying to get the school administration to do something, which is a very difficult option to pursue.

HER: How could we do that? I don't think we're working against her; we just don't like her.

It's wise to start talking about what the teacher's context for all of this might be.

YOU: You don't like her because of the way she yells at you and the way she teaches. Maybe you could tell her that she should work with you instead of against you. I know that probably won't work, but if a group of you talked to all the kids in the class and decided how you could make it a better place to be for all of you, including the teacher, and sent her an e-mail with all your ideas, maybe that would help. Tell her you'd like to discuss it with her. I think that would be the right thing to do and the best thing to do.

Involving the teacher in this means getting her to tell her side of the story so everyone knows where everyone else is coming from. It's also a highly ethical thing to do, giving the teacher your version and asking for hers.

HER: She would probably read the e-mail and go crazy. Then she'd yell even more.

She has hit on a real possibility.

YOU: That's a possibility. There's always a risk in everything we do. But could it make things worse for you? Things seem pretty bad already.

It could make the teacher target your daughter and her friends. Is it worth that risk?

> HER: I think you should take our e-mail and talk to the principal about the teacher and how we feel. That might be better for us.

At least the principal should hear about what's going on.

> YOU: That's a good idea. You get together with your class and write the e-mail to your teacher, copy it to me, and I'll talk to the principal about it.

It's good for you, as a parent, to get involved in this.

> HER: Great. Maybe this will turn out to be the right thing to do for all of us.

Conversations with Teens

Your teenagers' notions of right and wrong may be different from yours, but at their age, you can certainly have a good talk about it. They might watch the news or read newspapers and magazines that raise moral and ethical issues, and they can reason abstractly about these issues. They are certainly confronted by them everyday in high school, on television and the Internet, in movies, and in the stories about their musical and cultural heroes. Electronic games offer a veritable feast of ethical and moral issues as they allow players to steal and kill as a contest.

Because teens are confronted with so many issues because of their age and stage of physical, emotional, and cognitive development, the best approach might be a case study in which you pick out some news item that puts moral issues squarely in front of them.

Here's an issue that appeared in the news a few years ago. It raises some very difficult questions about human nature, moral responsibility, law, and justice. It's the story of the murder of an eleven-year-old girl by two boys, ages seven and eight, who then stole her bicycle. The police caught the boys. The court released them into their mother's custody, but ordered them to wear electronic monitoring devices. One of the questions now is what to do with these boys? Should seven- and eight-year-olds be held responsible for their actions?

We're used to stories of children killing other children and adults, but these killers are usually adolescents. That's why this situation seems so troubling. What can we say about seven- and eight-year-olds who kill?

The Choices and Moral Development Conversation Script for Teens

"We need to talk"

You've related this incident to your son and now you want to talk about the moral issues and lessons you both see raised by the killing.

YOU: What do you think about this case? I think it raises lots of issues about morality, about what we teach children, how much we hold them responsible for knowing right and wrong, and what we can do to stop the violence in this country.

Child violence is a great topic for you and your teens. It's current, important, and filled with moral and ethical issues.

HIM: It's a tough one. These were little kids. They don't know right and wrong at that age, do they? Did I? They're too young. They don't even know what killing or death really is.

He's raising many of the relevant issues, all of which are filled with questions about right and wrong. There may be no clear answers, but discussing them with your teen is wonderful.

YOU: One of the issues is, when do we think kids know right from wrong, because until we decide that, we can't decide what to do with them when they commit this kind of act. It's simple when they just steal a candy bar from the supermarket or take another child's toy, but to kill another child and then steal her bicycle—that's almost beyond belief.

The issue of when children are old enough to understand right from wrong in the same way adults do is at the center of the situation.

HIM: Yes, it sure is. I know that some religions would say kids that age should know right from wrong, but only at a pretty basic level.

We know that kids don't seem to understand it as we do. How, then, can they be held responsible for actions that presuppose that understanding?

YOU: Yes, Catholics believe in original sin, but even they would find it hard to believe an eight-year-old is capable of serious sin. One of the questions that comes out of this is how much we are born sinners and how much we learn from our parents and surroundings. If we're born that way, we can't be blamed for what we have no control over. Also, if we learn to do bad things from watching our parents or from people in our neighborhood, we can't be blamed even if we can be punished.

You're raising some important points that are at issue here.

HIM: It also then raises the question of free will. How free are we to make choices in our lives? I know I can't choose to be an astronaut and then become one without working very hard at it and having some degree of luck. But can I choose to rob someone or not to rob them, to kill them, or not to kill them? I think I can.

Talking about free will with your teen: nothing could be more fun, even though the issues are very serious in this case. What your teen is saying shows a nice depth of thought and understanding.

YOU: I think you can, too, but whether you do or not might depend on what you think the consequences of your actions might be. That's where we get into trouble in this case. Could those two boys really understand the consequences of their actions?

Much of the time, we're not sure that even teens understand the consequences of many of their actions.

HIM: I think some kids that age can understand what it means to kill someone and other kids can't. But that doesn't help because I don't know how I would know one kid from the other.

He's right. It's easy in hindsight to say children of the same age are different in their level of understanding, but all but impossible to predict.

YOU: Yes, that's a problem. They may understand in the abstract, but they don't understand in terms of real consequences.

This is the nub of the problem, which the courts have to decide, often with expert help that is often not so expert. But it's at the core of the discussion of moral behavior: If someone doesn't understand right and wrong, nor the consequences of their actions, they can't be held accountable for them even though they must suffer the consequences themselves.

HIM: We don't let kids that age do lots of things because we don't think they understand or are responsible enough. We don't let them drive, drink, smoke, own guns, sit on juries, vote in elections, or choose not go to school. If we think they understand and should be responsible for killing someone, then maybe we need to give them the rights that go along with such responsibilities.

Excellent points that many people overlook when confronted with child violence, including teen violence.

YOU: I think that's an excellent point.

HIM: So the question is, what do we really think about seven- and eight-year-old brains? Do they understand what killing is in terms of actions and consequences? I don't think they do. I think it's like them pulling the trigger on a gun without first seeing if it's loaded. They don't connect their actions with the consequences enough.

He's on a roll here, and we have to agree with his conclusions.

YOU: I agree with you. So the way to handle these two boys is to try to put them into a program that tests their understanding, and that equips them as they grow older with a good sense of right and wrong, of understanding the relationship between actions and consequences.

It's probably better than locking them up and leaving them to rot. Once they've undergone such a program, we can see where they and we stand on the issue of their understanding.

HIM: I agree.

"We need to talk"

Chapter 10

Separation and Divorce

DIVORCE IS A messy, painful business for all children, whatever their age. Grown children, as much as young ones, don't want their parents to split up, no matter what the reason. Your parents are always your parents and no others can take their place in your heart and mind.

That fact doesn't prevent men and women from separating and divorcing, and everyone will admit that it's sometimes for the best, especially for people in abusive relationships. When couples stay together for the sake of the children, it can prolong psychological and physical damage to a spouse and the children.

I, fortunately, have never been involved in a divorce of my own. One of my children has been divorced even after extensive marriage counseling, and my niece also divorced her first husband. In both cases the marriages were over almost as soon as they began and no children were involved. I have also experienced divorce among many of my acquaintances. In many of those cases there were children who had to be considered. And what happens to children in divorce paints a sorry picture because the child is always the victim as well as the bystander.

About three years ago I had an e-mail from a woman, whom I will call Eve, who had read my book on teens that included a chapter on talking to your teens about divorce. She was divorced and wanted my advice. Eve's daughter, whom I will call Rachel, was living with the father and refused to talk to her. Whenever Eve tried to contact Rachel by phone, she hung up. When she e-mailed her or texted her, Rachel didn't respond. Although they lived in the same town in Colorado, not far from each other, Rachel refused to visit Eve and wouldn't allow Eve to visit her.

Eve told me that Rachel started behaving this way when she and Rachel's father separated and got worse when Rachel moved out to live with her dad. Eve said Rachel was terribly upset by the separation and divorce and blamed her mother for it all. What could I advise Eve to do? How, she asked, could she open the lines of communication to try to restore the relationship that separation and divorce had all but destroyed?

I suggested that the best way to approach this was to arrange to a face-to-face meeting where she could have an open and frank conversation about this difficult subject. But to get to that point with a daughter who refuses to talk meant that she had first to lay her cards on the table, so to speak, in a way that Rachel would hopefully see. So I advised her either to e-mail Rachel, or to write a long letter to her in which she told her how she felt about the separation and divorce, how much she loved her daughter and how badly she wanted to renew their relationship.

In this way Rachel couldn't cut her off, couldn't argue with her, and words wouldn't be said in the heat of an argument that couldn't later be taken back. Rachel could, of course, not read the e-mail or letter, but Eve had no control over that and, as far as I could see, had no other options. Something in writing, I thought, also had the advantage of being there so that Rachel could choose to read it sooner or later and might at least be curious about what her mother had to say.

What I heard back from Eve delighted me, as it delighted her. Rachel had read her letter and called her mom. They had set up a meeting and Eve was hopeful that the relationship would be put back on track.

You can never be sure how your children will cope with or even understand your position regarding the relationship that is now ending or has already ended. One thing is certain, however: They will not understand it as you do! Whatever you say, whatever you do, your children will see it from their own perspective. Their parents, their home life, their love and security, the life they've taken for granted will never be the same. As I said earlier, this is true even for grownup children. You need to keep this in the front of your mind whenever you try to talk to your children about what's happening.

One more aspect of separation and divorce needs some attention because it can cause you even more problems than the actual ending of your marriage. Starting a new relationship can create a host of new difficulties for you in your relationship with your kids.

When you have ended a marriage and have finally gotten around to wanting a new relationship, you need to realize that slow is good for your children. Even months and years after a divorce, children will have a very hard time adjusting to a new man or woman in your life. If you are merely separated, the difficulties will be even greater. Your children don't want a new father or mother, or even the threat of one. No matter how sensitive you and your new interest are to the issues here, your children are unlikely to acknowledge or appreciate this sensitivity. That's why, if you value your relationship with your kids, you must go slowly.

Dating can be a minefield for your relationship with your child, so here are a few general rules: Go slow; talk about dating with your children before you start; get their view and ask for their advice, even if you find you can't follow it; don't say you're doing it for their sake; watch for signs of their reactions; steer clear of open affection and sexual displays in front of them; and, initially, keep your date out of the house.

Conversations with Preschoolers

The Swahili expression, polé, polé means "go slow." Literally translated, it means "slowly by slowly." That's the approach your conversation about separation and divorce should take with young children; they need time to adjust to this earth-shaking news. Although the cause of the separation may be real and justified, you can be sure your preschooler won't understand and won't sympathize. They want love, security, and for everything to remain the same—they don't like radical change.

Unfortunately, some statistics show that separation for couples with preschool children has grown considerably in the last thirty years or so, especially for those in common-law relationships. The legal entanglements of marriage seem to create a more stable bond between men and women and the statistics reflect that. However, staying together simply because it's hard to separate doesn't necessarily help the relationship or the child. Separation and divorce may often be best for all because of the physically and psychologically destructive forces that a bad relationship can set loose.

When separation and divorce seem inescapable, it's best that you know how to talk about it with your child to prepare them and give them the comfort they will sorely need.

The Separation and Divorce Conversation Script for Preschoolers

"We need to talk"

The most important things to emphasize in your conversation concern your child's need for reassurance that they are still loved, that you are not trying to find them a new mommy or daddy, and that things will change, but as little as possible. The worst thing you can do is bad-mouth your partner, trying to make your child choose between you.

YOU: I've got to tell you something you won't like.

No point in hiding the truth—it won't make things any easier—but keep it simple for your preschool child.

HER: What?

YOU: Things are going to change a little bit. Your daddy is going to be living someplace else for a little while.

This is one way of easing into it.

HER: Why?

Now you have to decide how much of the truth to tell. Remember the level of understanding and concern your child will have.

YOU: We think it will be better for everyone if he does.

This won't work too well at this age. You need to be more concrete.

HER: Why? I want Daddy to be here.

YOU: Daddy and I decided he needs to live someplace else.

It's good to make it a joint decision.

HER: Where is he going?

YOU: He won't be far away. He just won't be living here.

HER: I want my daddy here.

An understandable reaction.

YOU: You'll see him. He will see you every week.

Your child will need endless reassurance.

HER: I love my daddy.

YOU: And he loves you. And I love you, too.

You need to continue to say this.

HER: If he loves me why is he moving away?

A good, logical question which needs a good, understandable answer.

YOU: You won't understand this, but he's moving away because he loves you so much.

You're right, she won't understand this logic.

HER: No, he doesn't. If he loved me, he wouldn't leave me.

YOU: Your daddy and I both love you, but we don't have the same feelings for each other that we used to and we have to live separately.

This will be really hard for your child to understand, but what else can you say?

HER: No, you don't. I love you and I love daddy, and I want you both to live here.

YOU: We love you, but we can't live together anymore. You've heard us arguing all the time. We don't think that's good for you or for us so we've decided to spend a little time apart.

This is an explanation, but it can't fix the hurt and fear. Nothing can, so you're just doing your best.

> HER: How long before Daddy comes home?
>
> YOU: I can't say exactly. We'll have to wait and see what happens.
>
> HER: I don't want my daddy to go away.
>
> YOU: He's not going far. You'll see him on Saturdays and Sundays. He loves you and he wants to be with you.

It's very important to keep emphasizing this.

> HER: Why don't you love Daddy anymore?
>
> YOU: I do still love him, but in a different way than before, and we can't live together anymore because we fight all the time. It's not good for you to see us fighting. If Daddy lives somewhere else for a while, the fighting will stop.

A reasonable and truthful response your child is probably too young to understand. But that's the best anyone can do.

> HER: I want to see my daddy.
>
> YOU: You'll see him on Saturday. He's going to come and take you to the playground.

Good. Grounding it in specific, concrete days and details.

> HER: I want you to come, too.
>
> YOU: No, I'm going to stay here.
>
> HER: But I want you to come with Daddy and me.
>
> YOU: I think it's better if you go with Daddy and I stay here.
>
> HER: I don't think so.
>
> YOU: Daddy and I both love you and want to be with you. But you'll have to trust that what we're doing is the best thing for you and for us.

Don't let up on this. Just keep reassuring your child.

> **HER:** It's not best for me.
>
> **YOU:** You'll see, some day, that it is.

Conversations with School Children

For school children, one of the biggest problems separation and divorce poses is the likelihood that Mom or Dad will vanish from their lives. That can happen when the separation is filled with recriminations, strong emotions, and hostility between parents. Some experts suggest that when a parent leaves the home, the separation from their children is so painful they choose to cut off contact completely rather than having to suffer the trauma of seeing them and leaving them again and again.

One parent often blames the other for this choice, saying they sabotage the absent parent's relationship with the child by continuing to fight the divorce issues through the children, playing the blame game. High-conflict separation and divorce often shows this kind of ploy, using the child as a weapon against the ex-partner, seeking revenge by denying access to a child, or making access as difficult as possible.

If you love your child, you will not do this, not matter what your feelings toward your ex may be. You won't let your anger hurt your child by trying to enlist his help in punishing your ex. Mothers, far more than fathers, gain custody of children, especially preschool and school children. That gives mothers far more opportunity to influence the feelings of their child toward the father than the father does of influencing the child's feelings toward the mother.

Mothers have an opportunity to use the child as a means of revenge toward the father, destroying the child in the process, something many experts consider child abuse. School children look to parents to tell them whom they can and cannot trust. If either parent poisons a child's feelings for the other parent by teaching that Mom or Dad is dangerous or untrustworthy, that can do serious harm to the child's self-esteem because the child knows she is a product of both parents.

Don't let your resentment of your ex blind you to the need to do and say what's in the best interests of your child. Even though, as a mother, you may now have the lion's share of responsibility for raising your child because you have custody, you need to balance any anger you feel by asking yourself if you would give up custody to your ex simply to gain the freedom he now has. Even if you feel that you are the victim, don't let that feeling obscure your love for you child.

The Separation and Divorce Conversation Script for School Children

"We need to talk"

Here's a conversation you can have with your school child that may help you preserve your own self-esteem while showing your child he is loved and wanted by both his mom and dad, even though his world has been disrupted.

YOU: You know that your dad and I split up because we didn't love each other any more.

You've already been through the initial explanations.

HIM: Yes, I know that's what you said. But why don't you love each other any more?

At this age, your child deserves a reasonable story about why this has happened.

> **YOU:** We just found out that we didn't like the same things as much as we thought we did, and we didn't think the same way about life, or feel the same way about each other.

This is pretty good, even though your child won't really understand. Children generally don't, at any age.

> **HIM:** But you loved each other before. Why can't you love each other now?
>
> **YOU:** People change as they grow older and sometimes they change in different ways.

True, but no real solace for the child.

> **HIM:** But what about me? Do you feel differently about me?

This is a critical question.

> **YOU:** No, I love you more now than ever.

Good answer. You can never give too much love and reassurance.

> **HIM:** What about Daddy?
>
> **YOU:** He loves you, too.

Same as before, lots of reassurance needed.

> **HIM:** If he loves me and you love me, why can't you love each other?

A reasonable question from your child.

> **YOU:** We have fallen out of love, just like you stopped liking Patty in fifth grade.

This won't really be understood unless you can tie it to the child's experience.

HIM: Will you fall out of love with me?

If it can happen once, it can happen again.

YOU: No, I could never do that.

Keep saying that.

HIM: What about Daddy?

YOU: No, I don't think he could ever do that either. If you asked him, I'm sure that's what he would say.

This is a bit too tentative. You must reassure your child that both parents do and always will love him.

HIM: Why do you say bad things about Daddy?

Your child will never like to hear this kind of talk.

YOU: I don't mean to. It's just that sometimes I get very angry that he's not here to help.

Please don't, for your child's sake.

HIM: But then why did you send him away? If you didn't he would be here to help you now and you wouldn't be angry with him.

Can't fault this logic.

YOU: I didn't send him away. We agreed he had to leave because we couldn't agree on anything. If he hadn't left we would have just continued arguing about everything, and that's no good for any relationship.

It's good to make it a mutual decision.

HIM: Then why are you angry with him now when he's not here?

YOU: That's a good question, and it's one I don't have a good answer to. I was angry when he was here and I'm angry when he's not here. It's kind of crazy, but it's the way I feel. I think your father may feel that way, too.

You can be honest here. It's a terrible time for everyone and there's a lot of irrational thought and behavior possible.

HIM: When I'm with Daddy, he doesn't say he's angry. He doesn't say much except ask me about school and things.

YOU: Well, maybe it's because he doesn't have to look after you.

Try not to get testy. Your child just wants comfort and love and his parents not to fight.

HIM: Don't you like that?

YOU: Yes, of course I do. I love having you and looking after you. It's just that now I have to do it alone, when before your dad would help.

More reassurance.

HIM: Then ask him to come back, and he could help.

YOU: I'm afraid that's not going to happen.

HIM: I want you to be happy, not angry.

YOU: I am happy. I'm happy I have you because I love you very much.

Good ending.

Conversations with Teens

Teens can start making sense of separation and divorce for themselves. At least they've had fourteen or fifteen years, maybe more, of being raised by both parents. Being older, they are more attuned to the nature of the relationship between their parents that has now gone sour, and they can talk about it in a more sophisticated, rational way, than their younger siblings. But don't think that makes it any easier for them to accept. Understanding the troubles may give them a better insight into the reasons why their parents can't live together anymore, but it won't lessen the emotional blow, the anguish they will feel that the life they have been living will now disappear forever.

The same rules apply to conversations with teens about separation and divorce as apply to conversations with younger children. Avoid the blame game and recriminations, don't use your teen as a pawn in the disputes, don't think your teen wants a new mom or dad to replace the old one. Even teens who have escaped abusive relationships at home and are now in foster homes or under the care of social welfare agencies don't want new parents; they just want their old parents to change.

Teens can make up their own minds about whom to blame for separation and divorce, and they can also play the guilt card. But their object in this is not to inflict pain and suffering, but escape it by trying to shame or argue parents into getting back together. As futile an effort as that may be, it's a constant reality in a teen's mind when she has to cope with a parent who is no longer together.

The Separation and Divorce Conversation Script for Teens

"We need to talk"

The same issues arise in every separation and divorce—regardless of the age of the children—losing the old familiar patterns of relationships and way of life, and replacing it with new ways, routines, relationships, and patterns. Exactly how important these changes are will depend on the way parents relate to each other now and in the past—the family history and the rancor of the separation and divorce. Here's a conversation that deals with some of these issues.

YOU: You know that things are going to be different.

This will be inescapable and you might as well put it on the table.

HER: Yes, I know.

Your teen will cope better than your school child, but still not very well.

YOU: Things will be harder. We'll have less money and you'll have to help me much more than you did in the past, because your dad will no longer be here.

HER: I know. I'm really going to miss him even though I'll see him a lot.

Your teen can help you through this just as you can help her.

YOU: I know you will. I'll miss him, too, even though this had to happen. We just couldn't stay together any longer.

HER: I didn't really know there was a problem between you until Dad said he was moving out. You weren't fighting or arguing a lot, at least not when I was around.

This is a very sensible teen, no hysterics, no recriminations. That can happen in other situations.

YOU: No, it was a long time coming, very gradual, but coming nevertheless. We just couldn't go on pretending that things were the same.

HER: Was there another woman?

This can be an important issue. It can seriously affect your child, who will never want anyone to replace her mother or father.

YOU: No, not as far as I know. Your dad and I just weren't enjoying our life together anymore.

HER: Was it because of me?

This question needs a good, honest answer to make your teen feel secure and not guilty of anything.

YOU: No, never. How could you even think that? We both love you, always have, always will. No, it was just something that came between us, something we never thought about, just a drifting apart. We didn't enjoy doing things together anymore. He wanted to do one thing and I wanted to do something else. I think we stayed together as long as we did because we thought it was best for you, but now that you're older, we thought it wouldn't matter so much.

It's good to explain things at some length to your teen, who is certainly old enough to understand some of it.

HER: Well, it does. I can't imagine not having you and Dad here together, the three of us going out together, going on holidays, going to games and shows and movies, to restaurants and things.

Things will be different.

YOU: We can still do those things, you and I. And you can do them with your dad, but without me, I'm afraid.

HER: I don't like to think about that. It makes me cry. Why can't things just go back to the way they always were?

This is every child's wish.

YOU: I wish they could, but that's impossible.

HER: Can't you go to counseling or something like that to help you get back together?

YOU: We talked about it, but we decided we didn't want to go on together. It's just over. I'm sorry for you, but that's the way it's going to be from now on.

It seems pretty final, and you have to make that clear, even though it will take a very long time for your teen to accept it.

Chapter 11

Relationships with Other Children and Dating

FOUR YEARS AGO our entire family flew to South Florida to celebrate my father's ninety-fifth birthday. One day the weather wasn't good enough for the beach so we headed, with my grandchildren, for a nearby mall that I knew had a children's play area. There were four of them, two boys aged four and a half, and a boy aged two and a half and girl aged three.

The play area consisted of a variety of plastic shapes that the children could climb on, over, around and through, as well as slide on. There was a height limit so that most of the children were five or under. It was crowded with youngsters with parents watching carefully. I was watching too, anxious to keep our children safe and in good relationships with the others. That's when I saw a problem.

Our two-and-a-half year-old grandson was racing around the play area, having a great old time, but, in the process, pushing past others, sometimes pushing them physically out of the way, not waiting to take his turn, and generally being too aggressive, even with children much older and bigger. My son and daughter-in-law were very much aware of and concerned about this child's tendency to be too aggressive in his play with other kids, but I had never seen it in action in a public place.

But they knew what to do. They had seen this happen before and were working on socializing this little boy so he would stop his aggression, make friends and be considerate of his playmates. They knew that each time he displayed this kind of behavior they had to remove him from scene, sit him down and tell him what he was doing wrong, why it was wrong, and what the consequences would be for him if he didn't change.

Talking this way to such a young child is absolutely the right thing to do. Children, especially boys who may not be as verbal as girls at this age, tend to act out their thoughts, feelings and emotions because they can't put them into words. This was certainly the case with our grandson. He was a very late talker and did act out instead of trying to express himself in language. Yet he understood much more than he could say.

He is now six and a half and he has lots of friends, is very caring and not overly aggressive, and fits very well into his kindergarten class at school. His parents' strategy of removing him from the scene, talking, explaining, being firm and consistent has paid off handsomely. We also saw that as he became a fluent talker he stopped acting things out.

All children need to learn proper behavior toward others, especially in the early years. One of the biggest problems that can handicap children in nursery school, kindergarten, and first grade is the lack of proper social skills. Teachers want children in their classes who listen to directions, respect the rights of others, don't act out, and can express their thoughts in words. Boys often have difficulty with these skills, much more than girls, because girls' verbal abilities develop faster and at a younger age than boys'.

Proper behavior toward others must be taught to preschool children, but it doesn't stop there; all school children and teens need those skills as well. As play and other kinds of social interaction among preschool and very young school children moves from both sexes playing together to single-sex activities among older school children and early teens to increasing recognition of sexual differences and dating among older teens, parents must consistently monitor, teach, discuss, and model proper behavior toward others.

Role modeling concerns should be at the forefront of your mind when you think about your children and what they might be learning from you about how to relate to others in a positive and respectful way. Goodness knows there are enough movies, video and computer games, TV shows, and Internet sites that show how not to behave toward others. You want your children to respect the fact that while we all have personal rights and freedoms, we must respect others who also have those rights and freedoms. I would argue we need to consider the degree to which exercising our own rights will hurt others unnecessarily.

The basic issues are the same, whether your child is five and forming relationships with other kids in his school or fifteen and experiencing his first romantic relationship. They are respect and sensitivity toward other people's feelings, beliefs, personal identity, and personal safety. You need to talk to your boys about understanding and respecting girls and to your girls about understanding and respecting boys.

You will see when we get to our specific concern with teens and the kind of conversation you may want to have with them about this subject that you need to remember, as you already undoubtedly know, boys and girls have different starting points for dating, give the practice different meaning, and often have different goals and desires. Above all, remember that we're not talking about rational feelings or activities here. Much of dating has nothing to do with logic and reason; it concerns chemistry and biology motivating social rituals of courtship and mating.

Conversations with Preschoolers

You can never begin teaching your preschoolers how to relate to other children too early. In the same way we socialize dogs by taking them to obedience school, not just to make them obedient but to teach them how to interact with other dogs, big and small, male and female, old and young, we need to socialize our kids to get along with all other kids, big and small, male and female, old and young.

As I've said earlier, you need to teach your children to be considerate of other's feelings, to put themselves in someone else's place, and to treat others as they would want to be treated. This is all simple and straightforward, yet it's astounding how many parents fail to do it, just as so many dog owners fail to properly train and socialize their dogs. The key is persistence, consistency, explanation, and linking consequences to actions. This is where parents tend to fail. They don't persist or insist on proper behavior toward other children, they are not consistent in their rules, they don't explain why the rules and behavior are required, and they don't link consequences to behavior.

Preschool children have an emerging moral and ethical sense, and you have to help that develop by teaching right and wrong behavior toward other children. At this age, the teaching should be concrete. Don't do this, do that. This is wrong, this is right. This is why it's wrong, this is why it's right. These are the consequences for doing the wrong thing, these are the consequences for doing the right thing. Reward and punishment, within reason. And discussions of reasoning in simple terms about physical hurt, hurt feelings, or how you would feel if someone did that to you.

"We need to talk"

The Relationships with Other Children and Dating Conversation Script for Preschoolers

Here's a good conversation to have with your preschooler about how to behave toward other children on the playground, in school, or at play dates.

YOU: I was watching you just now and saw you push Mary and John out of the way so you could be first down the slide. That's why I've come to get you. Let's go sit over here where we can talk.

Always be specific in stating the problem.

HIM: But I want to play more.

He will take a while to accept that he was not behaving appropriately.

YOU: We have to talk first. You have to remember how to behave toward your friends.

It's good to have him try to remember these things.

HIM: But I do.

You can put him to the test.

YOU: I don't think so.
HIM: But I do so.

YOU: I saw you pushing John and Mary on the slide so you could be first. That's not right.

It's good to point out that his actions belie his words.

HIM: But they were too slow.

Of course he had a reason.

YOU: It doesn't matter how slow they were, it was their turn before yours, and you just pushed them out of the way and went ahead of them. That wasn't right; it wasn't the right thing to do.

You have to explain clearly and simply why his reason was unacceptable.

HIM: But they didn't mind.

His powers of empathy may not be highly developed.

YOU: How do you know they didn't mind? Did you ask them?

HIM: No.

YOU: Well then, you couldn't possibly have known.

HIM: But they didn't.

YOU: That's not really the issue. The issue is that you pushed them out of the way so you could go ahead of them and that's not good behavior. It has to stop.

Be firm and clear.

HIM: Why?

YOU: Because you have to treat other children in the same way you want them to treat you. Would you want Mary to push you out of the way so she could go ahead of you on the swing?

It's always worthwhile trying to get the child to empathize.

HIM: No, but she couldn't because I'm stronger.

YOU: That's not the issue. It's not a case of stronger. It's what is right and wrong. It's wrong for anyone to push someone else out of the way so they can go ahead of the person whose turn it is. You just can't do that. I won't allow it, and every time you do it I'm going to take you aside and remind you that it's not the right thing to do and give you a time-out so you can remember how a good boy behaves.

It's good to spell this out. Actions have consequences and bad actions have bad consequences.

HIM: But I want to go back and play.

YOU: Not until we sit here for a little while and talk. First, I want you to tell me what you did wrong and why I came and got you.

It's important for him to say it. If he can't, then you have good reason to believe he doesn't understand.

HIM: I pushed ahead of Mary and John.

YOU: Yes, that's right. Very good. Why was that the wrong thing to do?

Good question.

HIM: Because it was their turn before me.

Good answer.

YOU: Very good. You see, you know these things. I just have to keep reminding you. Can you tell me what the rule is?

It's important to acknowledge good answers.

HIM: It's wrong to push ahead of other children when it's their turn.

He knows how to say it. Now you must make sure he remembers it and behaves accordingly.

YOU: Excellent. What will happen if you do?

You're right to remind him of the consequences of his actions.

HIM: You'll come and take me away and have a time-out.

YOU: Exactly. Why will we have a time-out?

HIM: So I can remember the rule.

YOU: That's excellent. Now you can go back and play. And remember the rule.

Conversations with School Children

Relationships with other children are crucial to your school child's social and emotional development. He needs to know how to behave toward other boys and girls in order to be accepted by them, not rejected. It's especially important for your boys to learn how to behave toward girls in these predating years. The gender differences will become increasingly important, first as the boys-against-girls separation shows itself as a motivating force, then as boys and girls develop crushes on each other amidst shy talk and giggles and games of boys chasing girls and stealing hats and gloves.

All this preadolescent play serves as a prelude to the later, more serious, interplay of sex and social relations that leads to loving and lasting relationships. Teaching your children some rules of good relations with other children in school can come from good conversations based on real-life events and stories.

Gender differences being what they are, the approach you might take with boys will be different from that of girls when you talk about how relationships should be thought of and developed and how to show the other child respect. But there are also some good, general rules that boys and girls must both observe in relating to other school children.

The Relationships with Other Children and Dating Conversation Script for School Children

"We need to talk"

Here's a conversation you can think about that contains some general rules about these relationships, regardless of the gender of the kids involved.

YOU: Can we talk for a minute about some things I've heard from your teacher?

HIM: Sure. What things?

YOU: She told me that some sixth-grade kids were being picked on, really badly.

This can be a very serious issue if your child is involved as either victim or culprit.

HIM: So?

You need to get your child focused on this issue.

YOU: Is it true?

HIM: I guess.

He's being a bit evasive.

YOU: You only guess?

HIM: I know it's true.

YOU: What's happening? It seems really cruel and bad.

You've heard the teacher's story. Now it's time to hear your son's.

> **HIM:** It's not so bad. It's just that one kid gets picked out and the other kids tease him and say things about him and won't play with him and don't want to be in groups with him or sit near him.
>
> **YOU:** You think that's not so bad?

A reasonable question.

> **HIM:** It happens sometimes.
>
> **YOU:** Did it ever happen to you?

This is important to know.

> **HIM:** No.
>
> **YOU:** Would you want it to happen to you?
>
> **HIM:** No. Never.

That's a good answer.

> **YOU:** How would you feel if it did?
>
> **HIM:** Not good.
>
> **YOU:** How do they pick the kid who gets this treatment?

It will help your talk with your son if you learn about this.

> **HIM:** Some of the kids decide. Then the others go along with it.
>
> **YOU:** For any good reason?
>
> **HIM:** No reason. It's just we pick kids who aren't fun.
>
> **YOU:** Do you pick on these kids?
>
> **HIM:** A little, yeah.
>
> **YOU:** I think this is appalling. What do the teachers and the principal say about it?

It certainly is appalling and unacceptable.

HIM: Not much. I think they don't really notice it, except for my teacher and a few others.

YOU: Do you know what empathy means?

HIM: Yeah. It's when you imagine yourself in somebody else's place.

Not all children this age will be able to define it this well, but they should certainly understand it.

YOU: Do you ever empathize with the kids who are picked on?

HIM: Not much.

YOU: Why not?

HIM: 'Cause I don't think it would ever happen to me.

This is not an unusual attitude amongst kids.

YOU: I think we need to talk more about how to relate to your schoolmates and other people in general.

Yes, indeed you do. Your child needs a bit of an education on these matters.

HIM: Why?

YOU: You need to realize that causing others pain and suffering is wrong. It's a miserable thing to do and you should never be a part of it. Do you know why?

HIM: Because it could happen to me?

YOU: No, because if you allow it to happen to anyone then you are saying you don't care if it happens to you, or your family, or your friends, or anyone. What you and your friends are doing it picking on some kids because they're not like you, or they don't measure up to your ideals or standards, so they're not worthy of the same treatment you give to your friends. It's terrible. Do you understand?

Your child really needs to discuss this with you.

HIM: I guess. I never thought about it like that.

YOU: Then I think you better start thinking about it. And your friends, too. I'm going to talk to your teacher again and see what we can do to stop this.

This is a good idea. You do need to pursue it.

Conversations with Teens

I read a news article quoting an expert who runs a program in Colorado for young women who said she thought one in three teen girls experience physical, psychological, or emotional violence, either in the home or in dating relationships. The biological changes, emotional upheavals, and peer pressures that teens face all collude in some situations that overpower any thoughts about respect, independent thought, or self-worth.

More often than not, the girl is the victim of mistreatment when she seeks to justify her status among her friends by dating the "right" boy, whoever he may be and whatever kind of demands he might make of her.

Girls can also be guilty of abusing their boyfriends, not so much physically, but verbally and psychological, telling them how to dress, how to act, whom not to talk to, whom to have as friends— not the same degree of seriousness as boys abusing girls, but not a good thing nevertheless.

You can do a good job of protecting your teen from abusive relationships by modeling good ones yourself. Obviously, you don't want to abuse anyone in your family in any way, nor do you want to be seen or heard abusing others. Talking about relationships that are healthy and unhealthy with your teen can go a long way toward exposing anything that might be troubling her at any point. Give her practical hints on how to create and maintain good relationships, especially serious ones with a boy. Encourage her to tell you about her experiences, both good and bad. She will do this if you've developed an open, nonjudgmental relationship with her over the years.

Finally, make sure you know your teen's friends, especially any girl with whom he has a serious relationship. Make your home welcoming and friendly so your teen won't hesitate to have his friends drop by. Be alert for any signs of anger, hostility, or unkind treatment from others or from your teen. This will go a long way toward helping him have good, healthy relationships.

The Relationships with Other Children and Dating Conversation Script for Teens

"We need to talk"

Here's a brief conversation you can have with your teenage son to help ensure he will never abuse a girl with whom he has a relationship.

YOU: How is your relationship with Jane these days?

You need to monitor all your children's relationships.

HIM: It's good.

YOU: You're happy with it?

HIM: Yes, sure, why do you ask?

YOU: I've just been reading about teen relationships where the boy abuses the girl and I just wondered why any boy would do that, or why any girl would put up with it. Do you know any kids like that?

This is a very important issue; it's right to discuss it with your son.

HIM: Yes, I've seen a few. The boy can do pretty much anything he likes to the girl and she always comes back for more. I think it's crazy.

Terrible, but true.

YOU: Why do boys do that?

HIM: For some it's because they can. Or because they get jealous if their girl even looks at another guy. If she talks to him, her boyfriend will go ballistic.

It's useful to get your teen's version of this kind of relationship.

YOU: But why do the girls stay with these guys?

HIM: Maybe they're popular at school, on the football or basketball team. And they have lots of friends and lots of girls who'd like to go out with them. So their own girl feels important because their guy is important.

YOU: It doesn't sound very healthy. It sounds like both the boy and girl lack self-esteem. They don't have a good feeling about their own self-worth so they get it from the person they're going out with.

It's good for you to give your teen your view of things.

HIM: Yes, and they can get real angry with each other if something threatens that relationship. Even the girl. She lets herself be abused only because she's afraid of losing him.

YOU: You would never have a relationship like that, would you? One in which you abuse your girlfriend?

You want and should get reassurance on this from your son.

HIM: No, not me. I don't get angry very easily. And I certainly don't need to put down a girl to make myself feel big.

YOU: I was sure of that, but I wanted to ask you anyway. What do you think is the best kind of relationship with a girl?

It's important that you tell your son how you see and trust him.

HIM: I don't know for sure, but it's not hurting her or making her stay with you when she doesn't want to. I think for me, the biggest thing is love and respect. I would only want the best for her and hope she felt the same about me. And I would respect her, everything about her: the way she looks, talks, dresses, what she likes, who she likes. And I would treat her the way I want her to treat me.

All boys should learn this by heart.

YOU: Don't you think you'd disagree with her on some things or even argue or fight?

HIM: I'd never fight with her. We sure would disagree and argue, but I'd never physically fight with her. If she did that with me, I can't imagine why I'd like her.

YOU: What about sex?

This is not a topic most teens want to discuss with parents, but hopefully your relationship with your child allows for it to happen.

HIM: You really want me to talk about sex with my parent?

YOU: Not the details, I just want to know if you would ever make her have sex if she didn't want to?

HIM: Never. It wouldn't be right.

YOU: So, if I understand what you're saying, the biggest things for you in a relationship with a girl are loving and respecting her in every way. No real anger, even when you disagree. No physical fighting, no abuse, no trying to control her. She would be free to be her own person. Is that a fair statement of what you're saying?

It's good to provide the gist of what you've heard your son saying.

HIM: Yes. If I really loved her and she broke up with me, I'm sure I'd be crushed, but that wouldn't make me do anything to get back at her. At least, that's what I think now.

YOU: I realize you can't ever know what you'd do in a situation, but talking and thinking about it is like training yourself to do the right thing in any circumstance.

This is realistic, but hopefully your teen will always do the right thing.

HIM: That's a good way to think about it.

Chapter 12

Alcohol, Drugs, and Cigarettes

As PARENTS, WE would love to know how to protect our children from the scourges of alcohol and drug abuse and smoking. These substances represent different danger levels. For adults, alcohol, in moderation, seems to be healthy and actively prevents certain health conditions, according to the latest medical reports. Teetotalers, or those who abstain completely from alcohol, face a higher risk of heart attack than people who drink a serving of wine or spirits each day, especially red wine.

Drugs play an important and necessary part of our lives, particularly aspirin, muscle relaxants, painkillers, and therapeutic drugs prescribed by physicians. You may feel they help us control or ameliorate a wide range of symptoms and health conditions. We all know, however, that addiction to any drug poses a hazard to us, and addiction to illegal drugs like cocaine and heroin, as important as these drugs are in medical treatment of certain conditions, can kill us or land us in jail, not to speak of destroying our lives and the lives of those around us.

Nothing good can be said about smoking. Experts estimate that tobacco-related diseases kill approximately 1,200 people a day in the United States, or almost 440,000 people each year. Smoking is a major risk factor for heart attack, pulmonary disease, and cancers of the lungs, larynx, and mouth. It has also been linked to cancer of the breast, bladder, esophagus, kidney, pancreas, and stomach. Studies also link smoking to increased risk of respiratory ailments like colds and bronchitis. And the list goes on. You can drink alcohol responsibly and use drugs as prescribed or recommended for your health, but smoking offers no such options. It destroys the body and increases the risk of death by a high percentage. It directly affects the health of others who must breathe in second-hand smoke.

Obviously, the best and easiest way to begin teaching your children to avoid the addictive, destructive use of any of these substances is to set a good example for them. Don't smoke. If you do, then quit. It's very hard, but realize that you're doing it for your loved ones because it will keep you alive longer, which they would prefer. It will also keep them from your second-hand smoke, it will save money in health care, and it will show them you're serious about knowing and understanding the dangers of smoking. Many jurisdictions are passing laws that prohibit smoking in cars in which there are children—a good step forward.

Alcohol presents a much different set of issues that you and your children need to talk about. Some of you probably abstain from it completely for reasons of health, religion, weight loss, alcoholism, or any other reason. In this, you are setting an example for your children, but you have to decide how you want your children to drink or avoid drinking. Do you want them to abstain completely? For what reason? What will you do if they find social pressures too great when they reach the final years of high school?

If you drink, what are your habits? Do you drink too much? Can you control your drinking? Is there a history of alcoholism in your family? Do you drink in moderation? If you do, do you allow your school children, not your preschoolers, a little sip of wine or beer so they know the taste, then gradually allow them to have a little wine with dinner when they are teenagers so they learn to practice responsible drinking?

You have to decide what's best for you and your health and that of your children. But you should always do so with your children's well-being in mind. You don't want to be an example of a drug-dependent adult because you don't want them to grow up to be drug-dependent, either.

You don't want your kids to see you taking drugs just to wake you up, or put you to sleep, to make you feel happy, or to relieve a mild feeling of depression. You probably are already slightly addicted to coffee as a way to keep you going through the day. We live in a culture so saturated by drugs that it seems hard to imagine what life would be like without them.

Having said all this, there is one further aspect we need to consider that will help us make sense to our children and help us make sense of them. We need to talk to them about their well-being, about their sense of self and their happiness or unhappiness. Dependencies and addictions often come about as a result of low self-esteem, identity problems, emotional or mental illness, dissatisfaction with one's life, friends, status, appearance, self-image—the list goes on. You will want to talk to your child about substance dependency and abuse in the context of their lives; what they are feeling about themselves and others, how they like school, what friends they have, what makes them happy and unhappy, what they want and what they need, and how, in general they see their lives unfolding.

Above all, you want to help them feel self-confident, have a sense of self-worth and self-esteem, and be happy with themselves and with others. You want to help them understand that life's satisfactions are best found in good relationships with others and with oneself. They need to learn to find their answers to life's problems in themselves, rather than in a bottle, pill, or cigarette.

Conversations with Preschoolers

For preschools, this conversation is not about them using alcohol, drugs, and cigarettes, but a way to start dependency proofing them through early training and by being a good role model for them.

In the same way we began talking about teaching morality to children by suggesting we do a check of our own beliefs and behaviors, we can begin teaching abstinence of or moderation in drinking, moderation in prescription drug use, and abstinence of illegal drug use and smoking by asking ourselves questions about our own habits and dependencies on these things. Ask yourself a few questions:

~ Do you allow for drinking of alcohol?

~ If you drink, do you do so only in moderation?

~ Are you dependent on any kind of prescription or over-the-counter drug?

~ If you are, is that for health reasons or is the dependency more psychological than medical?

~ What is your attitude toward treating problems like stress, tension, anxiety, or sleeplessness with drugs?

~ Have you ever done illegal drugs?

~ Do you still do them?

~ What is your attitude toward drug users? Pushers?

~ Do you think all presently illegal drugs should remain so?

~ Would you legalize any presently illegal drugs?

~ Should drugs be treated in the same way as alcohol?

~ Have you ever smoked cigarettes?

~ Do you smoke now?

~ What is your attitude toward smokers?

~ How would you react if you discovered your child smoked cigarettes?

These are questions you should answer for yourself and discuss with your children, especially school children and teens. With preschoolers, you need to teach that alcohol is for grownups (they won't even like the taste of any hard liquor), and then only in small amounts.

You need to help preschoolers understand that when you or they take medicine, it's for a specific problem and usually because it's an acceptable remedy or a preventative measure. Unfortunately, this is not always the case. Research has shown that in some communities, children, especially boys as young as five, are prescribed behavioral-control drugs such as Ritalin and Dexedrine. There are strong arguments for and against using these drugs to control such things as attention deficit hyperactivity disorder (ADHD).

Your preschool child's regimen of vaccinations and inoculations are a good place to start with this education. You can explain they can't attend school unless they've had them, to protect themselves and other children.

The Alcohol, Drugs, and Cigarettes Conversation Script for Preschoolers

"We need to talk"

Here's a brief conversation you can have with your child about smoking. It's not an end; it's a beginning.

YOU: Did you see that boy smoking at the bus stop?

Good to use concrete examples.

HIM: Yes.

YOU: I bet he's just in high school. He shouldn't be smoking; it's so bad for you.

HIM: Why? When can you smoke?

YOU: You should never smoke. The things in cigarettes will kill you. That means you won't be you any more. You will be gone because the cigarette smoke will hurt you so much that you can't live anymore.

Hopefully this will be hammered home to him when he gets to school.

HIM: I don't want to smoke.

YOU: That's good. You should remember that always. When you're older, some people might want you to smoke, but you should always say no.

It's good to praise him for the right answers.

HIM: I will.

YOU: Good.

Conversations with School Children

Even if your children are still in elementary school, alcohol, drugs, and cigarettes can tempt them. Don't think it's only in poorer neighborhoods that young kids get preyed upon by older children and adults. It happens in the best of neighborhoods and in the best of schools, public and private.

You need to be vigilant and you need to have the kind of talking relationship with your child that allows all things to be discussed without fear. If your child knows there are terrible consequences for telling the truth about things he sees or does, he will lie to you, or even worse, not say anything at all. You probably know from your own experience which subjects you'd never talk about with your parents because they reacted so badly. You don't want your kids to learn the same lesson.

Once your child is in school, she will grow up much more quickly than you ever imagined she could, and will know much more than you will give her credit for knowing. On the other hand, she will still be innocent in a potentially wicked world and you need to protect her, giving her the knowledge and skills, and, above all, the self-esteem and self-confidence to protect herself in situations where temptations are great.

The Alcohol, Drugs, and Cigarettes Conversation Script for School Children

"We need to talk"

Here's a conversation that may help guard your child against making errors in judgment about what is good for them and what is not.

YOU: Did you see that boy smoking when we drove past the high school this morning?

HIM: Yes. I think he goes there.

YOU: You know how bad smoking is for you, don't you?

HIM: Yes, I do.

YOU: You would never smoke, I hope. I know a lot of high school kids do smoke. I see them outside the school smoking away, even when it's really cold. That's the problem with smoking, not only is it terrible for your lungs and all of the rest of you, it's an addiction. Once you start, it's very, very hard to quit.

You can't emphasize this enough.

HIM: I know. We had a film in health education that showed us what happens to lungs when you smoke. And we saw some people who had lung cancer. They started smoking when they were in school and thought it could never happen to them. Now they're probably going to die.

These films are great if they scare kids with images of what smoking can do.

YOU: I guess I don't have to convince you not to smoke. Do any of your friends ever sneak a cigarette from their parents?

It doesn't hurt to find out about his friends and the availability of cigarettes.

HIM: No, I don't think their parents smoke.

YOU: I'm really glad to hear it. As long as we're talking about this kind of thing, can I ask you about drugs? We're always worried someone will start peddling drugs in your school. We've heard about this going on in some elementary schools before.

Drugs are, perhaps, the most serious issue and concern for parents.

HIM: I don't know any kid who takes any kind of drugs, except some boys in my grade who are hyperactive. They get stuff from their doctors and the teachers make sure they take it.

Your child will be familiar with these things.

YOU: Are these boys your friends?

HIM: One is. He says its okay to take it because it makes him less jumpy and he can think better. He doesn't need to move around all the time.

YOU: That's probably Ritalin he's taking. I've heard a lot about it.

HIM: I don't know about any other drugs, but I heard some grade-two kids took some sleeping pills from one kid's mom and were all sleepy in class, so the principal called the EMS who took care of them and found out they'd taken the mom's pills.

YOU: That's scary! Parents really have to be careful with their medications and keep them away from kids. You can kill yourself if you take too many sleeping pills.

HIM: Yes, I heard.

YOU: Well, now that we're on a roll, what about alcohol? Do any of your fifth-grade friends sneak beer or wine from their parents?

It's important to learn of his knowledge and experiences.

HIM: Yes, some do. But I wouldn't drink it. I know you've let me have a little taste of beer and wine and that's okay, but I don't really like it.

YOU: I'm glad. I don't want you to think that we think alcohol is a very bad thing, like drugs or cigarettes, but it can be really bad if you drink too much, or you can't help yourself and can't stop. We have a word for that. We call people who have to drink and can't stop alcoholics. It's an addiction, like smoking, and they say people who are alcoholics are always alcoholics, even if they never take another drink. It's a way of getting them to protect themselves from thinking they can start drinking again and not overdo it.

A good closing statement, but it won't end here. You need to keep up this conversation until he's grown up.

Conversations with Teens

For teens, the conversation probably works best if you talk about substance abuse in general first and zero in on anything that specifically concerns you. We all know that teens have many opportunities, as well as pressure on them, to do things that fall into the category we call risk taking. Boys are especially vulnerable to peer pressure when it comes to risky behavior. They are out to prove their manhood to their peers, the girls they want to impress, and themselves.

Substance abuse may not be as immediately risky as crazy stunts, reckless driving, daredevil sports, and rough-and-tumble behavior, but it can be more dangerous in both the long and short term, and both boys and girls are prone to it. That's why it makes sense for you to spend time talking to your teen about how to cope with the dangers of easy access to alcohol, drugs, and cigarettes and the many opportunities that present themselves that can change their lives and yours from happiness to sorrow.

One expert recommends prepping your teen with a repertoire of ways to say no to offers of drinks, drugs, and smokes which, through practice and repetition, become automatic responses that can be used in every situation. The threat is real, so the training must seem real, too. Role playing can simulate this reality. Although it might feel strange and a little forced at the beginning, it can open the window to many serious discussions of dangerous possibilities. It's certainly a way to start talking.

The expert suggests imagining all the "what ifs" you can, and gives the following examples: "What if somebody's parent wants to drive you home and they've been drinking?" "What if a friend offers you drugs?" "What if you get to a party and find kids drinking?" You can imagine many more what ifs that suit your own family situation. Clearly, they can be used for almost any eventuality. It's a great way to help your kids make good decisions.

The Alcohol, Drugs, and Cigarettes Conversation Script for Teens

"We need to talk"

The following script presents some practical ways for you to engage your teen with this idea of pre-scripted responses they can use whenever they feel they need to.

> **YOU:** Let's do that role-playing exercise I told you about.

This is really worth doing.

> **HER:** Oh, that seems so silly.

It may take a while for your teen to buy into this.

> **YOU:** I know it seems silly, but humor me and try to get into it. I'll go first. Imagine you're at a party and a friend comes up and says, "I've got some weed. Want a smoke?" What would you say?

You can show that you understand her feelings. Then show her she's not prepared for the occasion if it should present itself.

> **HER:** I don't know.

> **YOU:** You see, you need to know how to react, almost without thinking. Your answer has to be automatic.

That's the goal.

> **HER:** I see. Okay, I would say, "Sure, I'd love to try some."

A little humor and teasing is good.

YOU: No! That's the wrong answer. You're supposed to say, "No, my parents would kill me." Now, be serious.

You can be the serious one.

HER: Okay. "No, my parents would kill me."

YOU: That's good. Now I'll try another. Your boyfriend calls you and says, "I've got some beer hidden in the garage. Come over and we'll have a little party." What do you say?

HER: "I love a good party!"

This is good, she's into it; her teasing shows that.

YOU: Wrong. You say, "My parents don't allow me to drink until I'm of legal age and I respect their wishes."

HER: "My parents don't want me to drink until I'm legal age, and that's okay by me."

YOU: That's good. Now let's try one more. You're walking home with some girlfriends and one offers you a cigarette and says, "Try this. It looks so cool and it gives you something to do with your hands." What would you say?

HER: "I think kids who smoke are jerks. It makes everything smell bad—your hair, clothes, breath and everything. It's also incredibly bad for you."

This is a great response. Let's hope she'd really use it. If only all kids thought this way.

YOU: That's a great answer. Much better than the one I had in mind. Do you want to do any others?

HER: No thanks, I think I'm getting the message.

YOU: The point is will others get your message? Your answers have to be automatic, no hesitation, no opening that some other kid will try to use to get through your defenses.

HER: I understand. I've got the answers down pat. "No, my parents would kill me." "No, I won't drink until I'm legal age." "No, I think kids who smoke are jerks."

YOU: Sounds good to me.

And it is good. Now, let's hope it works!

Index